Born by the
River

Born by the River

The true story of a young girl growing up along the
Mississippi River during the summer of 1963

JENNESS CLARK

ISBN: 0692797525
ISBN 13: 9780692797525
Library of Congress Control Number: 2016911359
The Big Muddy River Press*Imprint

*In memory of all those who came before me
and for those who will come after.*

Jenness Clark, the author, in 1959
With her right foot in Illinois and left foot in Missouri

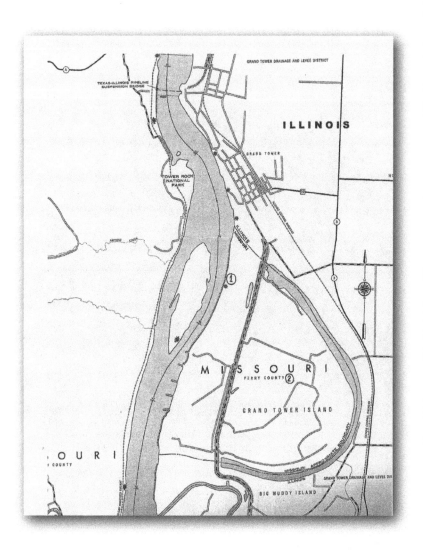

Wilson Family

Frank Wilson (b. 1872) m. Nettie Berry Wilson (b. 1872)
|
Lola M. Wilson (b. 1894)   Price Wilson (b. 1900)
m. Elbert L. (Wamp) Poe
|
Marion F. Poe (b. 1924)
m. Cyrus F. Clark, Jr.
|
Elizabeth Jenness Clark (b. 1951)

Poe Family

Charles F. Poe (b. 1864) m. Mary Jane Sumner (b. 1875)
|
Elbert (Wamp) L. Poe (b. 1895)
m. Lola M. Wilson
|
Marion Francis Poe (b. 1924)
m. Cyrus F. Clark, Jr.
|
Elizabeth Jenness Clark (b. 1951)

Clark Family

Cyrus F. Clark (b. 1847) m. Sophia M. Roth (b.1869)

Margaretha Arnold	Elizabeth Jenness	Cyrus F. Clark, Jr.
b. 1908	b. 1910	b. 1911
		m. Marion Poe Paul

Elizabeth Jenness Clark
b. 1951

Roth Family

Adam Roth (b. 1826) m. Margaretha Arnold (b. 1837)

Sophia Margaretha Roth
b. 1869

Preface

When I was in high school, I found a notebook in the living room of the house where my mother and I lived in Taylorville, Illinois. On the first page, written out in my mother's beautiful handwriting, were the words, "The Island has always been a part of my life." I knew right away it was the first line of a book she hoped to write about the island on the Mississippi River that had been our home. As far as I know, that was the only sentence she ever wrote about it.

Now, almost fifty years later and with a lot of help from her, I have written my version of the story. It's mostly set along the Mississippi River in southern Missouri and Illinois during the summer of 1963. I was twelve years old.

I felt the need to write this with two voices: one written in italics, as a child telling the story during the time period, and the other in normal font, as an adult reflecting back. The book is written with two different outlooks from the viewpoint of the same person. I believe memory works that way. We remember what happened and how we felt at the time, and then we apply hindsight so that we can explain it to ourselves.

The island and its nearby towns of Grand Tower, Illinois, and Wittenberg, Missouri, have always been a part of my life and always will be. They rest in my mind and linger in my spirit.

One

Now and then we had a hope that if we lived and were good, God would permit us to be pirates.

—MARK TWAIN

The summer of 1963 marked the last time I would cross the river with Uncle Price.

On that first morning in June, we crested the levee in his truck and looked down over the river. There it was waiting for me, the Mississippi. Seeing the river that day, the worries about my family back home seemed to float off downstream and disappear around the bend. The heat hanging over the land also vanished when we drove down to the water, as clouds from the Missouri side were making their way east with the promise of a cooler afternoon. Maybe it was on account of my lighter heart, but all of a sudden everything looked different; it was like my world had changed in some way. Then it dawned on me—I'd just finished grade school and would start junior high in the fall. I wasn't a kid anymore. I guess you could say that graduating from the sixth grade made me officially a grown-up—at least that's how it felt.

Once at the landing, we unloaded Uncle Price's truck and carried his gear down to the riverbank.

We always put in under the shadow of Devil's Bake Oven, the ninety-foot limestone rock that looms over the east side of the Mississippi just north of Grand Tower, Illinois. Dank caves at the edge of the rock look down on the river and overflow with stories about Indian bands hiding out there as they tried to stand their ground against the first settlers. Pirates also used the caverns for hideaways while they waited for boats to ambush, and if you're brave enough to walk to the back of a cave, you can still smell their musky odor. Around Grand Tower, strong currents and whirlpools are created by bends in the river and rocks that squeeze into the water along both sides of the shoreline. That part of the Mississippi has a reputation for being one of its most dangerous stretches, and in the old days it was known as a good place for a surprise attack since the river both narrows and turns in the same spot. Devil's Bake Oven was a perfect lookout to see what was coming at you from around the bend.

I felt like it was my lucky day when Uncle Price said he needed to mend his fishing nets before we set out—the extra time would give me a chance to climb up to the top of Devil's Bake Oven and look out over the river. If you had any imagination at all, it was the best place in the world to play. I made my way up to the top of the rock and stood at the edge of the cliff to study the current. A plan for ambushing flatboats and rafts that were heading downstream from Saint Louis started to form in my mind while I watched the water swirl below me. Then looking upriver, I squinted just right and saw something appear in the waves just after the turn—it was a raft. With only three men onboard it would be easy to take, and right next to me on the knoll was the perfect stick to use for a weapon. I grabbed it and ran down the path to jump into my skiff. If I pointed my boat to the right spot in the river, the currents would work for me, and that unlucky raft headed downstream would be ambushed in no time.

After a while I gave up being a pirate and made my way over to everybody's favorite spot on Devil's Bake Oven—the overgrown ruins of an old house that were on the flat plateau of the rock.

Everybody in town knew the story about a young girl named Esmerelda and her father who used to live there. We knew about Esmerelda's life the way we learned the name of our town—without remembering where we heard it. They said that when Esmerelda and her father first came to Grand Tower, her dad let her choose the place for their home—in the end she picked the top of Devil's Bake Oven rock. He was a rich man and wanted everybody to know it, so they built a big house that loomed over the river. It was the golden age of the Mississippi, before the Civil War, when all kinds of boats landed at the town as they traveled up and down the river. Before roads and railroads, Jenkins Landing in Grand Tower served as a main stop along the river, where goods could move in and out of the area. Lime, coal, livestock, and corn were sold downriver, and everything that came from the rest of the world was brought up from New Orleans. Jenkins had a woodyard for steamboats, so most of them stopped there for fuel.

Esmerelda's father had made some money from those boom times and was powerful around town; everybody knew he was looking for a rich man for his daughter to marry. After a while he made up his mind that he'd found just the right person for her; however, his choice was an older man, and she didn't want anything to do with him. His age might have only been an excuse, though, because by that time Esmeralda had a few plans of her own—she'd fallen in love with a young pilot from a riverboat called the *Spectre*.

I walked along the foundation of the old mansion and thought about her standing watch over the river—she'd probably looked from this very spot while she waited for his boat to come around the bend. I retraced her footsteps on the path that led from the house down to the landing and felt the force of the Mississippi all mixed up with the danger of their forbidden romance.

She must have sensed that danger in her bones, too, but that fear didn't affect her plans. In the end she got caught when her dad started to notice something fishy was going on. He locked her away in their house—but in my mind it was a great tower with a large wooden door. At the top of the tower she looked out and saw the *Spectre* go by as it traveled up and down the river—her heart breaking when she watched it pass. We were told her father was relieved and happy and that he'd even chuckled when he heard the news that the boiler on the *Spectre* had exploded and killed the young man.

I walked to the edge of the rocks and imagined what it would've been like to jump. Could she have made it out far enough to land in the river? The story was that she'd gone straight into the whirlpools, but that didn't seem likely on account of all the rocks that were right below me—she couldn't have cleared the cliff. I leaned over a little more to see which rock she might've hit but was startled when a chill passed through me—it felt like somebody had just walked over my grave. Glancing around, I expected to see her standing on the path that led up to the old foundation where we all knew Esmeralda still walked, but all I saw for sure was a vanishing shadow that passed over some rocks and a bush rustling in the still morning air.

Looking back, now I can see that Esmerelda's tragic end and her lost hopes mirrored the sad stories that were about to unfold in my own family over the next few months. My parents were rapidly losing their grip on life—they were starting to slip under, and in the next few years I would come close to going down with them. Family problems were beginning to surface like water moccasins trying to find something to slither onto. That spring was the first time I felt the troubles that had been rising around me for years—just like Esmerelda, my world was about to drown in its own sorrows.

But on that first day of summer in June, I was looking across the river and getting ready to forget the problems back home. I was on my way to visit my grandmother, and that was just about the best place on earth. Summer was here, and I'd be passing my time in heaven.

Pretty soon I was done going over everything on Devil's Bake Oven and looked down to check on Uncle Price. He was finished with his nets and had moved on to adjusting the engine, so it was time to put in. I was halfway down the rock when he called out, "Come on now, Missy. It's time to go!"

Then I was thrilled to hear him add, "Hurry up, we're going down to Tower Rock to check the nets!"

Uncle Price was one of my mother's people. During the eighteenth century, some of them had migrated west on the Wilderness Road that ran from Virginia through the Cumberland Gap; others came later on the Cumberland Road. They earned their keep as farmers and rivermen. In the early part of the twentieth century, they settled on both sides of the river in southern Missouri and Illinois, but today they're mostly found in Walker Hill Cemetery near Grand Tower. Two miles south of the town is the island that was my home, and across the river on the Missouri side was my great-grandfather Frank Wilson's farm. You couldn't see his house from Grand Tower, but before the Mississippi claimed it, the tin roof used to sparkle in the sun when you looked across the river from Devil's Bake Oven. I spent a good part of my summers at Grandpa Wilson's farm and usually crossed in a small skiff with my great-uncle Price.

Sitting in the front of his little boat, I watched him push out far enough into the water to drop the engine and pull on the starter. As we set out, the river looked like glass and was deceivingly still and placid.

Even in dangerous areas, like the spots with the most whirlpools, there is always a calmness to the surface of the water, and you almost never see white caps. This smooth and shiny façade always gave me a foreboding feeling— with the river you can never forget that the danger is in the undercurrent.

Together, we motored along downriver past the park and then the town of Grand Tower.

The little river town feels more like a small whirlpool in the water than any part of the land. Bluffs to the east of the river valley look like a natural wall against the rest of Illinois, but the hills that rise over the basin aren't the only reason the town has drifted through time isolated from its surroundings. The people of Grand Tower have always been different from others to the east because the town was founded by settlers coming upriver from Kentucky and Tennessee—not overland on wagons from New England. When people came north on the Mississippi, a unique way of life formed along both sides of the narrow strip of land that stretches from New Orleans to Hannibal and beyond. Before there were roads, the river highway united people along its banks, and a culture was born. These men and women—black, white, and Indian—were connected by the Mississippi and shared their customs and traditions as if they were all part of the same place.

I grew up on an island in the river and even went home as a newborn in a skiff, but my only memories of being on the Mississippi were the times I spent in a boat with my great-uncle Price Wilson. He was one of ten siblings of my maternal grandmother, Lola Wilson Poe. By the early 1960s I had five great-uncles living in the area—three on the Illinois side in Grand Tower and two across the river in Missouri near my great-grandfather's farm. My great-uncles were mostly a good-natured group of men who were comfortable on both the river and the land. I passed a lot of time in their houses and never once heard them swear or say an unkind thing about anybody. As far as I knew, they all worked hard, didn't drink, and took good care of their families. Mostly they wore denim overalls, had soft cackling laughs, and liked to "pull your leg" as they called it. With them, sweet teasing was as common as sweet tea—it was part of every conversation, and the children in the family were easy targets.

Born by the River

Uncle Price had me sit in the front of his boat while he manned the noisy outboard motor, so there wasn't much talking while we were on the river. I turned my head around to look at him every few minutes and felt reassured by his easygoing smile—I felt safe on the river with Uncle Price.

In a habit that was common in the family, he always assigned me an important task to keep me busy. On the river, my most fun job was to keep a lookout for water moccasins and dead bodies that might be floating downstream. Water moccasins were plentiful along the shores; however, to my great disappointment, dead bodies were few and far between. I had to be satisfied with Uncle Price's embroidered tales of finding them, and the stories came alive easily when I spotted floating logs and branches that looked like corpses.

"Don't pull 'em in by the hair, now. Their hair will fall off if they've been in the water too long," he called out when I pointed to a log.

"Has that ever happened to you?" I yelled back, but I already knew the answer since I'd asked this question so many times before.

"Only once. It was a girl with long dark hair—kinda like yours. Women always float facedown, you know." He was shouting over the motor. "Men float faceup."

I was left with the vision of myself floating facedown in the river with my hair gently swaying around my dead body. We kids were used to the teasing though, so my mind quickly came back to the practical instruction of how to handle a corpse in the river. It was good to know these things in case I had to hop to it.

Uncle Price cut the engine, and we started to slow down; I knew the teasing was done for the time being. We were coming up to Tower Rock and getting closer to its whirlpools, so he had to pay attention to how the water was moving. I steadied my feet on the bottom of the boat and turned a little bit to fix my eyes on the hundred-foot monolith that sits like an island on the Missouri side of the river.

Early photograph of Tower Rock

Today people climb up to the top of Tower Rock, but back then most of us would never have thought about doing anything so foolish. We were part of a line of people connected to the early settlers who'd heard the stories told by Native Americans from around the area. In those legends, the Indians warned of demons living on the rock—demons who would reach out and pull you into the whirlpools and currents swirling around the tower. It wasn't hard to imagine those stories were true because you always felt something strong whenever you even looked at Tower Rock—never mind being near it on a boat. But along with the fear and wonder for that part of the river, there came an equal amount of love; if you lived around those parts, you had a personal tie to Tower Rock. All of us habitually studied it from the riverbank while we meditated on the power of the water swirling around the base. For some reason or other, no matter how many times you've seen it before, Tower Rock never fails to surprise you. There are always a few seconds of silence and astonishment that follow after your eyes first take it in, and you can't help but think it's an amazing thing that such a rock is out there by itself in the river. I probably saw it a thousand times growing up and almost never failed to feel relief to see that it had survived through the night. Sometimes Tower Rock's steadfastness was one of the few things I could count on, and being up close to it in the water always bore out its mightiness and venerability to me.

Born by the River

Uncle Price turned the skiff just right so he could get to the nets and then he put the engine in idle; while he was maneuvering the boat I watched the whirlpools swirling around the base of the rock where the water was hammering away at the narrow limestone shoreline. Looking at the turbulence in front of me, it seemed like the Mississippi was on a rampage to wipe Tower Rock off the face of the earth. The river had lost that fight for thousands of years, but it's hard to think of another fight—any fight—the Mississippi had ever lost.

"The river's up," he said, studying the water level.

No other spot gives you the chance to gauge the height and current of the river the way Tower Rock does.

I tried to take it all in as we sat there in the quiet little place he'd found for us in the water while he fussed with his nets—whirlpools swirled around on one side, and the current of the river's main channel passed by on the other side.

I couldn't tell if I was in heaven or on my way there what with all that was going on—there was a tension in the air between the danger of the river and the beauty of our surroundings. Pretty soon my mind started to drift off to some of the legends about the area that I liked to think about. I looked up to the trees on the top of the rock and tried to find the place where the Jesuits had put their white cross in 1698. They were trying to prove to the Indians that there weren't any evil spirits living there; none of us would ever believe that for a minute.

"Uncle Price, where do you think the Chickasaw Indians killed those twelve Frenchmen?" I asked. But he was going through his nets and didn't answer me.

Then my favorite legend came to mind—the wedding party that had drowned in the whirlpools right before the Civil War. But just then a big bird flew by us, so I thought about something my Aunt Liz had told me about a man named John James Audubon and how he'd seen a young bald eagle resting up in a tree when he passed by the rock in a keelboat. He didn't know what kind of bird it was because he'd never seen a young eagle before, so he named it the "Bird of Washington." She also told me that Lewis and Clark had stopped there to camp in 1803 as they made their way upriver to begin their journey west. Clark was so impressed by the dangerous waters that he made a sketch in his journal. In those days, before they blasted out some of the rocks in the river, people had to come ashore and pull their keels and barges through the currents using ropes while they walked along the bank.

My people felt a tie to that place because it was the heart of our world. After all, we lived in Grand Tower, and this was Tower Rock—but it was more than just something to name a town after. We all knew that if the rock hadn't drawn in the first settlers, our town wouldn't be there. And without the town, many couples, including my own parents, wouldn't have met and created the new families that lived there for so many generations. So while we weren't dependent on Tower Rock for survival, the fact remained that we wouldn't exist without it. The monolith gave us something beautiful and powerful to look at plus a little inspiration to try to make a living along the river. Like the rock itself, the town had fought more than one battle with the Mississippi and maybe survived a few fights. But we all knew the river would win in the end. As Mark Twain said, "The Mississippi River will always have its own way."

Looking at Tower Rock from the shoreline was always awe inspiring, but coming up to it in a boat never failed to put the fear of God in you. That turbulent stretch of the river marked the end of the last wooden-hulled, packet-style sternwheeler when the *Golden Eagle* ran aground on the towhead of our island on May 18, 1947. It was the first voyage of the season, and the steamboat was headed south from Saint Louis to Nashville. Most of the ninety-one passengers were still asleep when the bow of the boat, all beautifully trimmed out with gingerbread woodwork, got stuck on the sandbar. The paddle wheel quickly sank into the river as the crystal chandeliers swung sideways—they would never grace the dining room of an elegant riverboat again. Everybody survived; my dad was one of the men who helped the passengers onto a towboat that took them into Grand Tower. Then they boarded a bus and were taken back up to Saint Louis.

According to the rules of the river, the boat could be salvaged once the captain abandoned it, so the townspeople quickly piled into their skiffs and started dismantling the beautiful *Golden Eagle* before the river got it. Liquor, food, and cigarettes were the first to go, and to this day the green deck chairs can still be spotted on porches and in backyards around town. One of my cousins found a case of cigarettes onboard—he was only about ten, so he hid them away in a shed behind his house. In the end, a lot of boys around Grand Tower started smoking because the *Golden Eagle* had run aground. With the last wooden-hulled passenger boat on the Mississippi sinking, it was the end of the most glorious era on the river.

The sinking of the *Golden Eagle*, May 18, 1947

One thing everybody from around those parts understands is that being near Tower Rock on the water is serious business—when I was growing up, the closest I ever came to danger was in a boat near the whirlpools that swirl around the base of the rock. For people living along the river, the Mississippi is mysterious and beautiful. But none of us were swept away by its splendor more than once—if you had to learn that lesson the hard way, you usually didn't survive to tell it. All our families did their best to scare the living daylights out of us when it came to the river. I can't remember ever seeing anybody swim in it because we were warned over and over again about the dangers. We all knew that if a whirlpool didn't suck you down, a giant catfish might eat you. Big ones that would bite your leg off were part of our myths, and every once in a while, a giant ugly one would end up being touted around town at the end of a hook to prove the story. In a boat you feared the eddies, currents, and whirlpools— and along the shore you were afraid of the quicksand. But if those warnings didn't put the fear of God in you, all the stories about drowned relatives and friends scared us enough to make sure we stayed put on the riverbank. I was told that my grandmother got her nickname "Bill" when she was drowning in the river and a black man by that name pulled her out. My mother always said that she was never the same after she saw her ten-year-old cousin, Frankie, drown while they were together on the Missouri side. All the drowning stories ended the same way—with talk about the bodies and their recovery. Did they ever find them? And if so, where were they? In

Frankie's case they found him about twenty-five miles down-river by Cape Girardeau, Missouri—he was floating faceup, of course. Living on the river shaped us—the respect we had for the Mississippi went a long way in explaining why we were such cautious and observant people who understood that fate always has to take its course.

Pretty soon Uncle Price stood up and pulled in his hoop net.

"We got us a few," he said. "Looky here."

He sorted out some trash from the river while three good-size catfish flopped around inside the net. Then he slipped them into the bottom of the boat and reset his nets back into the water. Catfish don't flop around too much, so I wasn't worried about them biting me, but they sure are ugly to look at. I was hoping we wouldn't have to eat them for dinner, until the Hush Puppies came to mind.

It wasn't too long before we were headed back upriver toward the sandbar that was in front of Grandpa Wilson's farm. I was relieved to be moving away from Tower Rock and turned back one last time to look for the ghosts of Penelope, John, and the rest of them. Sometimes if the light was just right you could make out their figures hovering over a swirling whirlpool.

"It'll be a hundred and twenty-five years next year," Uncle Price said, reading my mind. We both took a long hard look at the

monolithic rock and the whirlpools around it. That's right, I thought, doing the math in my head; it was April 9, 1839.

A wedding party of about ten people from Grand Tower crossed the river that day so the bride and groom could get married on the tower. Among the group, Penelope Pike was the bride, and John Randolph Davis was the groom. The bride's parents and sister were also there, along with the groom's mother, the Reverend Josiah Maxwell, and a few oarsmen. After the ceremony, the party started back across the river, and soon their boat became trapped in the current.

I looked at the swirling yet glassy water that hovered next to the lowest part of the rock where they would have tied up the boat.

After setting out, the rowers realized their boat was in trouble and panicked. Then a whirlpool started to spin them around, and everybody screamed for help. The swirling water twisted the boat in a circle as the river pulled them under. In the end, they all drowned except for a young black man who was rescued in the middle of the river by some fishermen.

On that same day, the groom's brother and his wife had a baby girl in Grand Tower—a birth that probably saved them from going to the wedding and ending up dead like all the others. The emotional turmoil of having such a tragic thing happen at the same time as a baby was born must have been overwhelming for the whole town. How fitting it seemed that in honor of the dead, the new father and mother named their baby Penelope after the bride.

Studying the rock again, I wondered why, twenty-one years later, the younger Penelope and her family decided to come back to Tower Rock to celebrate her birthday—anybody with the sense God gave a goose would've known better than to do a stupid thing like that.

It happened after the party was over, and they were in the boat on their way home. They were starting to feel relieved and congratulated themselves for putting the past behind them once and for all since, in a way, they had cheated death itself. But those smug feelings sank faster than the skiff had twenty-one years earlier because suddenly the wedding party rose up out of the whirlpools in the river. No words were spoken, but it was said that the dead Reverend Maxwell handed them a scroll and then returned to the river. When they read the scroll it prophesied that a great war would soon divide the country and that father would fight against son and brother against brother. Two years later, the Civil War was declared, and the younger Penelope's two brothers volunteered—Noah with the South and Thomas with the North. On August 10, 1861, both brothers were at Wilson's Creek near Springfield, Missouri, when Thomas was shot at while he was on picket duty. After he returned the fire he heard a man yell out, and a chill swept over him when he recognized the voice. I guess he probably heard that cry for the rest of his life because Thomas had just killed his own brother, Noah.

My thoughts about that tragedy faded as our boat made its way back upriver, and we saw the sandbar in front of Grandpa Wilson's farm. After we landed the boat, I grabbed my little suitcase and climbed up the riverbank to the railroad tracks that ran between the farm and the river. My ears perked up at the sound of a train coming, but I knew I'd be off the tracks and in the vegetable garden before it got close enough to hurt me, and life was suddenly too good to worry about a stupid old train. Halfway down the garden path I looked up to see Grandma waiting for me on the porch. She had a big smile on her face, and her hands were clasped at her waist—I knew she was as thrilled to see me as I was her. She would have been looking out for us from the time we drove up to the riverbank on the Illinois side in Uncle Price's pickup truck, and then she would have watched to see if we were coming straight over or stopping to check the nets. After that she'd probably waited on the porch until we were safely back from Tower Rock.

Once in the house, neither one of us thought much about Uncle Price because we knew he would follow along in his own good time after he took care of the boat. Then he'd spend the rest of the day tending to some chores on the farm, but before he'd go back across he would come and sit with us on the porch to visit and watch the river for a while. Watching the river was something we all had to do every day.

Two

For time is the longest distance between two places.

—TENNESSEE WILLIAMS

If I didn't go to Grandpa Wilson's house by boat, my mother would have to drive me around to his farm. That would mean sitting in the car for over an hour and a half while we drove down to the bridge at Cape Girardeau and then back up north to Wittenberg, Missouri, instead of a fun ride across the river with Uncle Price. Sometimes my older sister would come with us since our parents wouldn't let her stay out on the island alone. But by this time she was old enough to want to spend time with her friends in town. On the island, it was mostly just the four of us living by ourselves a mile and a half from our nearest neighbor, unless we had a tenant farmer staying in the house on the other side of the horse pasture. We had no electricity or telephone on the island, so we made do with a generator that got turned on in the morning and off at night, and there were lots of trips into town to use other people's phones. Years ago the channel of the Mississippi shifted and moved the island from its legal address in Missouri to a new spot next to the Illinois side.

In the 1950s, a big lawsuit between the two states decided once and for all what state it would be in. Since Missouri won, the island was officially in that state. Daddy was very happy about the outcome because if Illinois had won, we wouldn't have owned the place any longer. When I was growing up, if my parents wanted to vote or had any kind of legal business, we had to find our way to the Illinois side and then drive to a bridge at either Chester or Cape Girardeau. After that we drove around to the spot directly across the river in Missouri. The good news was that this took about an hour and a half each way for both us and the game warden from Perry County, Missouri. Needless to say, the hunting seasons on the island were often illegally extended beyond the regular legal time frames. But my dad always said that hunters were the best conservationists since they maintained the forests and the animal populations more than anybody else. He lived that philosophy by not clearing over two thousand acres of woods on the island. He hunted deer and waterfowl, but his favorite sport was coon hunting, and he did it as often as he could.

In 1953 the Army Corps of Engineers finished a levee across the tip of the island from the Illinois side. After it was built we had a land bridge to the rest of the world, so life got a lot easier for us. But if we wanted to see Grandma, we had to drive around to the Wilson farm where she lived with her dad, or we had to go by boat with Uncle Price. Grandpa Wilson's farm was about half a mile south of Wittenberg, Missouri. As I think back to the drive, the trip flies by in a blur because my mother always drove as fast as she could, and it didn't matter to her one bit whether she was driving on a highway or a dirt road. "Like a bat out of hell," Daddy would always say—it was the only time I ever heard him swear. He would grumble about her fast driving every year as he bought her another new car because she'd burned "the rear end" out of the old one. Her fast driving was hard for him to understand since he always drove at a snail's pace in his old Ford pickup.

When we drove to Wittenberg we usually crossed the bridge at Cape Girardeau. After Cape Girardeau the road came inland for a few meandering miles over rolling hills and past prim little farms on the Missouri side of the river— they were pretty, if we could catch a glimpse of them as we raced along. The people living on those farms were mostly Germans, and their orderly ways contrasted with my mother's family—the Scottish and English settlers who'd come from the south through Virginia, North Carolina, Tennessee, and Kentucky, to live in the river-bottom lands. Over the years there was very little mixing between the two groups—mostly they kept to themselves while holding their ground. The Germans were quick to call us "river rats," and our people liked to ridicule them for their orderliness.

It was always a relief when Mother had to slow down her driving as we neared the river. The countryside changed there. The neat little farms and rolling fields disappeared, and the road began to curve and wind through hollows and over creeks. In those rocky hills the houses looked run-down, and you could tell that most of the people living there were poor—life was hard on the Missouri side of the river because the soil wasn't as rich as on the Illinois side.

Once in Wittenberg we passed the town's small, white-washed, one-room schoolhouse with its bell tower and out-house. I always turned my head to look at it for as long as I could while we drove by. The little building was interest-ing to me because it was my real grade school, since this was the official district of the island—sometimes I felt like I belonged there instead of at the grade school in Grand Tower, Illinois, where I was enrolled. One time I went inside to see what it looked like and was amazed by how well or-ganized everything was. All eight grades were in one room, and there was a simple friendliness to the place. But lickety-split, we always passed it by too fast and went flying around the turn at Uncle Woodrow's house. Then we sped past Grandpa Wilson's mailbox and barreled down the dirt lane that led to the river and the farm. When the road ended the car plopped down in a pile of dust as my mother came to a screeching halt behind Grandpa Wilson's house. I al-ways felt like we'd just run into a wall, since suddenly every-thing around us was so still and quiet—it always seemed like two different worlds crashed together when Mother was on Grandpa Wilson's place.

There was a calmness about that farm that was missing from my real home on the island. People back home were always contentious with one another—that separated us and made me feel lonely. And with a family always at odds there isn't much peacefulness or security. Here on the farm I had the love and sanctuary of my grandmother, plus we were connected to the rest of the world by first the train track that ran at the edge of the front yard and then, after a few feet, there was the river that was just about the biggest freeway in America. I never felt lonely there. Later on in life I learned there were some troubles on the farm, but as a child I wasn't drawn into them. Grandpa Wilson was an old widower, and he and his daughter, my grandma, lived there together by necessity not by choice—divorced and alone in the world, it had fallen on her to move into her father's house after her mother became sick. Years later I often wondered why my grandmother had given up the life she loved in Grand Tower to stay on and keep house for her dad after her mother died. After all, my grandmother had four children who could have helped sort out a different plan for her father's care. Her youngest son, Edgar Allen Poe, was a riverboat captain, which was the top of the heap in those parts. Her other son, Rainey, was a single man with a good job who lived next door to the house she owned in Grand Tower. Nettie, her oldest daughter, lived in California, and everybody always said she was well off. Yet she moved away after she got married and never came back. Her other daughter was my mother, Marion. But for whatever reason, after Grandma Wilson died, my grandma stayed across the river to live with her dad. I could tell she didn't like being there because sometimes when we sat on the porch and looked out over the river toward the town she would talk sadly about the life she left behind. As far as I know she never went back to visit Grand Tower in all the ten years she lived with Grandpa Wilson. Later on when I asked family members why she made that choice, I was always told the same story: that it was expected of her, and if you knew Grandpa Wilson you wouldn't need to ask why. Family members explained that she never really had a choice at all. I knew in my heart that what they said was true because of Grandpa Wilson's disposition, and each summer I saw how she lived under his will—he ruled the roost, as they say. There was a bleak harshness to the life she started on his farm at the age of sixty-four—she spent her time tending the chickens, milking the cow, churning butter, slopping hogs, and growing food in the garden that she then canned. All this work was done just to feed her and her dad, but her difficulties weren't something anybody noticed at the time. Nobody in the family ever seemed to think much about her.

For the rest of the summer my world started at the mailbox in front of Uncle Woodrow's house and ended on the sandbar of the Mississippi River that ran along the east side of the property. Behind the house and to the north, hills rose, and on the south side of the farm, ponds and trees dotted the pastures. The lane that wound from the mailbox to the river was a quarter mile long and bordered pigsties, an orchard, and two ponds. At the end of the gravel road, you were in their back yard. The first thing I always noticed there was a big butcher block with a dip chiseled out of the middle. The chunk of wood was where chickens were fixed for eating—after their heads were chopped off and they'd had a good run around the yard. Off to the left was a stone smokehouse that sat deserted—by that time they were only using the cellar as a place to store vegetables; nobody was smoking hams there anymore. A sad, old persimmon tree kept the smokehouse shaded all summer. Out back and up the hill was an outhouse that Grandpa Wilson still used, which was a good thing since it seemed like the only time he ever left the house. A little past there and down the hill was the chicken coop and the barn. These were all well-worn buildings that needed paint or repair because in September 1963, Grandpa Wilson would turn ninety-one.

The main house, a little tin-roofed cabin, seemed old to me, but everybody always called it "the new place." It was probably just twelve to fifteen years old at the time of my first memory there. I'd been told my whole life that the old place burned down in 1946, and then Grandpa Wilson and his sons built this smaller house. But the idea of something different ever being there never really sank in for me. Around that time they didn't need a big house anymore because their nine sons and two daughters had died, grown up, or moved away. The old place was a beautiful, white colonial building, and it had stood out as a marker to pilots traveling on the narrow section of the river. The rivermen in the family said that it signaled danger was coming up ahead, and the pilot needed to beware of Devil's Backbone on the left and Tower Rock on the right as the boat came around the bend. It was said that when the house burned down, more than one pilot was a little thrown off as he looked out for it while he navigated his boat up or down the river. No one ever said that the new house, a quaint little cabin with a tin roof that sloped down over an open porch, was ever used as a marker for riverboats.

If we had driven there in the car, Mother would come inside, and we would sit in the front room for a few minutes to visit with Grandma and Great-Grandpa Wilson. It always felt like a false time of conversation making with the creaking sounds of rocking chairs covering up what would go unsaid. But the awkward time soon passed because after a few minutes my mother would get in her car again and leave us in a pile of dust and fury that settled silently. Then the rituals of the life my grandma and my great-grandfather led would set in for me—a life that centered on the upkeep of animals and the age-old customs of a traditional farm.

Things never changed there because Great-Grandpa Wilson was born on a farm in Missouri in 1872 and didn't know any other way of life. For him it would have seemed like nonsense not to keep a cow or chickens. How would you eat without a vegetable garden, and what would you do with your garbage if you didn't have a hog to feed in the pen? He was a descendant of over eight generations of farmers from Westmoreland County, Virginia—their earliest farms bordered the plantation of George Washington's grandfather, Lawrence Washington. Grandpa Wilson's direct ancestors, the Spens, were James Monroe's great-great-grandparents, and Robert E. Lee was born on land they had owned a hundred years before his birth. His people were from Scotland and England. They were Cavaliers who, as Royalists, had fled England after Charles I was beheaded in 1649. Their resettlement in Virginia was a lot like the Puritan migration that had happened twenty years earlier when Charles I dissolved the parliament. After Oliver Cromwell fired back for the Puritan side and beheaded Charles I, it was the Royalists' turn to escape to America. Since the Puritans had already claimed New England, they came to Virginia. The Puritans' and Cavaliers' animosity for each other would rear its ugly head again three hundred years later in my own family when my mother and father married—I guess time didn't change things too much. Grandpa Wilson's people were Pate, Wren, Hallowes, Youell, Shepard, Doling, Ethell, Haney, Sanford, Sturman, Spens, and Wilson. They always put kinship first and fought in any war or against any Indian they could find. Being quick to fight back was a trait they'd picked up in Scotland, where they'd had to battle it out for survival against the Romans, the Vikings, and then the English. When the West opened up after the Revolutionary War, they left Virginia, and three more generations of his people passed through Tennessee and then to Audrain County, Missouri.

Back in Virginia, they'd learned the hard way that farming tobacco brings down the quality of the soil; after a few years of growing it planters needed new land. Because Grandpa Wilson's family started out as tobacco farmers, they'd gotten into the habit of clearing land, farming it, and then moving on to the next place—this was unlike their German neighbors who made a home and stayed put. Grandpa Wilson always held tightly to the traits of his early kin because he had kept their lifestyle of starting a farm and then pulling up roots—this was the third or fourth place he'd settled. It seemed like he clung to a lot from his past. Even his speech had a trace of Scottish brogue, and he would use words like "lad" and "lassie" when he called out to us. His Virginia ancestors decided things for themselves before the Revolutionary War, and like them he steadfastly refused to let anybody tell him what to do—especially the government or a preacher. He had a stubborn pride that served him well in his old age because it milked a little extra respect from the people around him.

If there was ever a situation he didn't understand, Grandpa Wilson would study it quietly until a plan formed in his mind—you could see that on his face when he squinted his eyes and drew his head back a little. A simple thing like asking somebody for information would have to be carefully thought out before he would ask it. You could see him wondering: *How much weakness would I be showing if I asked that question, and if I got an answer that was useful to me, would it count as a favor? Would I be obliged to this person, and what would I have to give them in return?* It was all part of a fierce distrust of strangers that had been inbred for over a thousand years. We were brought up to believe that you almost never asked a favor because the only person you would have had to ask was a stranger—everybody else already knew you, and most likely they would have figured out what you needed and given it to you before you knew what had happened. According to his rules, you didn't take the shirt off somebody's back unless you were willing to give yours, but he would have done anything for a family member in need. There was a powerful obligation to give to our own people balanced with a fierce requirement to distrust strangers. What you ended up with was hard for outsiders to understand. They were a people who were known for their generosity to one another on one hand and the strong desire not to be beholden to outsiders on the other; they were hospitable to strangers, but things could turn on a dime into resentment and a fight. Grandpa Wilson was the oldest person I knew, and he was our connection to those customs—he was the patriarch of the Wilson clan, and that meant something to us. But although he was loved and respected by all of us, I was afraid of him. To me his nature was grouchy, contentious, and stubborn. I saw him as somebody who was always quick to start an argument and had to have everything his own way.

Those traits were common in Missouri during the aftermath of the Civil War, and he may have learned them firsthand from some of the people who'd survived the fighting. One of his favorite boyhood stories was about the day he and his dad were over at a neighbor's farm sharpening their axes, and suddenly a gang of men galloped in on horses. He was thrilled to watch their antics as they raced up and down the lane and then rode around through the trees while they fired their guns at makeshift targets here and there.

The man who lived on the farm got a kick out of seeing the shocked look on his face. He said, "You better close your mouth boy, or you'll catch a fly. You're looking at Jesse and Frank James, and don't ye ever forget it."

Grandpa Wilson talked about that day for the rest of his life—from then on he idolized Jesse James and wouldn't let anybody say a word against him. He got it into his head that Jesse robbed from the rich and gave to the poor; he was so set on venerating him that it made you think he saw the James gang give the neighbors something valuable. Pretty soon after that, Grandpa Wilson started going by his middle name, Frank.

Over the years he had made friends with the train conductors in Wittenberg when he sold his eggs and butter in town. As the trains traveled back and forth from Saint Louis to Memphis, the conductors got into the habit of throwing their newspapers off the train in front of his house. One day, a cousin of mine got fed up with hearing about Jesses James—he was also tired of fetching the newspapers out by the railroad tracks. To have a little fun, he slipped an unbecoming article about the James gang into the *Post-Dispatch*, but Grandpa Wilson figured out pretty fast that the article wasn't part of the paper. Before the day was done, he'd given my cousin a talking-to for almost three hours.

"I never want to hear another word agin Jesse James," he said. "He was a great man who robbed from the rich and gave to the poor. I saw it for myself, and I'm here to tell you about it. Do you understand that, boy?"

Nobody argued with Grandpa Wilson for long; it was always easier to run away as fast as you could.

Grandpa Wilson's wife, Nettie Berry Wilson, was the youngest of Mary Yager Berry and Henry Louis Berry's nine children. They were of the Berry family from Culpepper County, Virginia. Her father had been married before and had another nine children from that marriage, so I guess you could say she was the youngest of eighteen. She was born Henrietta Berry in Audrain County, Missouri in 1873 and married Frank Wilson at the age of nineteen. Her family was German and, like Grandpa Wilson, Scottish and English. They settled in Virginia in the early eighteenth century—they were Fischer, Yager, Blankenbaker, Berry, and Finks of Captain Marc Finks who fought in the Revolutionary War.

In 1956 when Grandma Wilson got sick my grandmother, Lola Wilson Poe, moved onto the farm to care for her parents. Two years later, Grandma Wilson was dead, and from that time on, everything in the house was still placed exactly where Grandma Wilson had left it—nothing changed after she passed away, and there was never much of an imprint of my grandmother on the place. Because of Grandpa Wilson's mean disposition, I always imagined that he had bullied his wife and ruled over things with her the way he did with his daughter, but as I grew up and started to wonder about Great-Grandma Wilson, I learned that she was known as the domineering, ornery one in the family. It was said that she decided what was what. This wasn't out of the ordinary, though, because it was common in families from that area for the matriarch to have all the power. My great-uncles, who were her own sons, always recoiled and shook their heads when her name came up and said something like, "She was somebody you didn't want to cross." Then talking to one another and over my head, they would tell a story or two about her. "Remember how mad she'd get if you happened to walk into the kitchen at the wrong time or if you didn't come when she called?"

Evidently, she had a real temper and didn't like it if someone disturbed her when she was washing her hair or if you ate something you weren't supposed to. She was a strict Southern Baptist who wouldn't tolerate playing cards, dancing, or smoking, but her sons managed to hide their cigarettes in the barn, and Grandpa Wilson was known to walk into Wittenberg every day for a beer. The spirit of Grandma Wilson stayed in the house long after she was gone.

My great-uncles, all eight of them, always had the same way of talking about anything—they would say something, nod, and then chuckle or shake their heads. For them there was no need to tell a complete story because they'd heard them all a hundred times. The purpose of speaking was not to retell the story but to reminisce about it and then to remember the person who was dead or the situation that was past. A pause and a little silence would always follow after a talk about anybody who had died. Because of this habit you only heard bits and pieces of what happened, and then you had to put it together later on by yourself. Asking questions wouldn't help because then the leg pulling would start, and before you knew it a tall tale would get woven through—and you might get caught up in it. In the "show me" state you learned not to believe everything you heard because people were always teasing one another.

Frank Wilson's house, 1956

Frank Wilson and Nettie Berry Wilson with sons, circa 1946

Even without a tall tale, though, I don't think I always heard the whole truth about things when I was growing up. Most people told me what they thought was the truth or what they wanted the truth to be. Or sometimes they'd say something that reflected well on themselves. In the end I had to sort it out the best way I could. But figuring things out was hard because children don't have the perspective to see what's really going on around them. With hindsight I've been able to look back and figure out what happened, and it helped to have a little love and understanding in my own heart. In the beginning I saw them as perfect, in the middle they were all flawed, and by the end I realized they were just human. After some time, when I began to understand where they'd come from and what they'd experienced in their own lives, I started to see why they did what they did.

Three

Life is all memory, except for that one
present moment that goes by you so
quickly you hardly catch it going.

—TENNESSEE WILLIAMS

*T*he stifling humidity and heat seeped into my dreams before I
woke up on that first morning at the farm. I was used to sleeping in different places because I passed so much time at other people's
houses, so it always took me a few minutes to adjust and figure out
where I was. It was a relief to hear the sounds of flies buzzing around
the bedroom and remember I was at Grandma's. Drifting in and out
of consciousness, I spent some time watching them meander around
the screen and then crisscross their way back toward the door. Then
I turned over to check Grandma's bed—it was empty. Everybody
else must be awake. I looked back at the flies, but they were repeat-
ing themselves, so my thoughts drifted off to the cold biscuits and
apple butter that would be waiting for me downstairs. Most likely
Grandma would be standing at the sink with the table behind her set

for my breakfast; she would be done with the milking by now, and it would be separating in large earthenware bowls on the table in the dining room. Grandpa Wilson would be fixed in his rocking chair in the front room with his spittoon to his right and his bed to the left. He would stay there for most of the day. I knew when I came downstairs, Grandma would say, "Would you like a scrambled egg, honey?"

And then, without knowing it, I would slide willingly into the timeless rhythm of the farm. Without a thought about a calendar or a clock, life would unfold in the well-regulated manner that had been preordained for decades.

I remember the farm mostly by recalling pieces of it, not by thinking back to the many events that happened there. In the front of the house and facing the river was a downstairs bedroom where Grandma and I took naps in the afternoon, and on the other side of the staircase was the front room that also faced the river. It had a small black-and-white television set that kept us updated on the farm report every day at noon; next to the TV there was a side table with a party-line telephone that never seemed to ring our particular ring. In one corner of the front room was the potbellied stove with a wood pile next to it, and in another corner was a beautiful rolltop desk that had an infinite amount of cubbies. That desk and a set of marbles helped me pass many long hours on the farm. There was no sofa in the room, only chairs and a small cot that had been moved in for Grandpa Wilson. I never knew why he wouldn't sleep in the downstairs bedroom that was just a few feet away from his favorite rocking chair. It probably had something to do with his stubbornness. Most of the problems on the farm were attributed to Grandpa Wilson's stubbornness. One time I remember my Grandma wanted to redo the wallpaper in the front room, but of course Grandpa Wilson thought this was frivolous. Grandma got one of her brothers to help her, and together they hung the paper on a very hot and humid day in August. Pretty soon, to put an end to what he thought was foolishness, Grandpa Wilson got it into his head to start a blazing fire in the stove. Before too long, the paper started slowly peeling off the walls with the sticky, wet glue dripping down in globs. Nobody said a word about it—we all just sat there watching it peel away. Later on, one of my great-uncles said it was proof that he was the most stubborn man who had ever lived.

After eating my breakfast that morning, I decided to go around the house to make sure everything was still the same. Sure enough, the dining room hadn't changed a bit since the last time I was there. I ran my finger around the rim of the milk bowls, which were setting out on the big mahogany table that took up most of the room. A thin layer of cream was just about ready for skimming.

I can only remember eating in the dining room once: that was when some people we didn't know very well came for dinner. All the other meals were taken at the big table in the middle of the kitchen. The kitchen was the best room in the house because it was Grandma's, and that was where all the good things happened. Grandpa Wilson came in for meals, but he only stayed long enough to eat—then he was back in his rocker, where he sat twiddling his thumbs and chewing tobacco all day.

The kitchen table was covered with a floral oilcloth, and we used it as both our eating table and a workplace between meals. Like most farmhouse kitchens at that time, another floral pattern decorated the linoleum floor. Nothing in this room ever changed and that gave me a wonderful sense of security. It felt good to know that everything always stayed the same there.

After making sure the dining room was all right, I spent the rest of the morning going around the kitchen to check on things. I started with the stove; next to the stove was the icebox. After that was the washstand, where I paused to look at myself in the mirror that hung on the wall above it—everybody but Grandma always washed their hands there before they sat down to eat. I dipped my hands into the water and worked up a big lather of soap that made my hands look like they were encased in beautiful white gloves—they looked like fairy gloves. My next stop was a bowl of water with a ladle in case you were thirsty. I took a little sip of water and then carefully hooked the end of the ladle back over the edge of the bowl, so it wouldn't slide down. After that was the cabinet where the flour was stored—inside the cabinet door was the sifter that was built in just under where the flour was—Grandma never used that sifter, so it seemed pretty rusty.

While I was checking on things, Grandma was at the stove where she was starting to cook our midday meal.

"Can I sift the flour when you make the cornbread for dinner?" I asked her.

"Yes, honey. That would be nice." She turned around and gave me a big smile.

Then I hurried past the sink as fast as I could. It wasn't fun to be near that part of the kitchen ever since the time when I'd found a big rattlesnake in the cabinet underneath it. But I was excited about the next stop because it was my favorite—an old water pump that nobody ever used. Of course, I always made sure it still worked every time I visited, but it seemed like you had to pump it forever before any water came out. After the pump, the last thing to check was the table where the electric butter churn was kept—we only used that one day a week. When I was done going around the room it felt good to know everything was still in its same place and that nothing had changed.

"Grandma, have you found any snakes in the house lately?" I asked.

"Not many," she answered. But it didn't seem like she was giving me the whole truth, since she didn't look up from her bowl when she answered me. I knew for myself they were everywhere.

Just in the house alone, I'd found one in my bed, while I sat in the living room I saw one crawl through the window, and I came across another in the bathroom behind the toilet—not to mention the rattler under the sink in the kitchen. In the chicken coop, they went after the eggs, and in the barn they ate the mice; before we went swimming in the pond we threw rocks in to scare them off. More than once, in my rambles through the hills behind the house, I'd come across men from the local university who were looking for snakes—they made me feel important when they asked me questions about what snakes I'd seen lately. They said we had the largest variety of snakes in the United States, and that made me proud of where we lived. I never got bit by one, so they didn't bother me too much—that is, until one day when I was walking down the railroad tracks from Wittenberg to the farm. I was with a cousin, and along the way we found a little baby rabbit hiding next to the rail—I brought it home and put him in a box in the utility room. The next morning my rabbit was missing. Looking around the room for him, I found a big snake stretched out against the wall with a lump in it. Pretty soon tears welled up in my eyes and started to flow without me knowing where they came from. It was horrible to think about where my rabbit was and to know that I'd never see him again. But, then again, he was still in the room and only a few feet from the nice home we'd made for him. It took me some time to figure it all out. Pretty soon, Grandma had me back in the kitchen where I stood listening to the commotion in the utility room.

After a few minutes she said, "Well, that snake is dead." Then she put her arms around me and leaned down into my face. "Honey, I need you to help me out today and go down to get the mail."

I remember nodding and swallowing hard—getting the mail was a job of mine, so I had to pull myself together. Once in a while the postman dropped off something, and in those days anything in the mailbox was important, so I needed to concentrate on holding on to it all the way back home. A stop at the pigsty to look at the little piglets would have to happen on the way to the mailbox, not on the way back home.

"The cherry tree is full, and the ladder is out there. If I gave you a sack, could you bring me back some cherries? You could put the mail in the sack too. It won't hurt anything if the envelopes get stained." I understood what she was saying, and it was a relief to think about something besides my rabbit.

Grandma always gave me lots of jobs around the farm, and completing them made me feel good about myself. Getting the mail was one of the most exciting things to do because it was an adventurous walk past the two pigsties, a pond, and then the orchard—at the end of the lane was the mailbox. It was a quarter of a mile, which was the perfect distance for a walk, especially since there was so much to see on that little country lane. Other jobs I had were helping her with the milking, feeding the chickens, and gathering the eggs. On washday I helped with the wringer, and on butter-making day I helped with the churn and then took Grandpa Wilson his glass of buttermilk. The only time we ever got into a car was every two weeks or so when Uncle Cy, one of my grandmother's brothers, drove us into Perryville to buy groceries. Grandma was always happy to go, and she got ready by wearing her best dress and spending some extra time on her hair. We would stay a couple of hours in the town, and each trip included a visit to the drugstore, where I had my first fountain Coke with crushed ice. One year she discovered Tang at the grocery store in Perryville, and it pleased her to no end. When she found premade biscuits at the store, she started sneaking them onto the breakfast table—I promised not to tell Grandpa Wilson we were feeding them to him, and he never noticed the difference.

Back in the old days, when Grandpa Wilson first settled in Wittenberg it was a thriving little hamlet, and you could buy groceries there, but when I was spending my summers on the farm, the town only had a population of around twenty. Grandpa Wilson used to make fun of the Germans who settled in the place—he always said that after they landed on the riverbank they marched up and down the sandbar in lockstep. In 1963 there was still a tavern in the town where you get a Coke and play pool, and it even had an old bomb shelter within the city limits. But that was about all there was to the town of Wittenberg. Grandpa Wilson had a brother who lived there, and every once in a while he would walk the quarter mile from town to the farm for a visit—we always had a lot of relatives stop by during the summer. Grandma's brothers worked the farm, so they would pass through sometimes and sit for a while. If their wives came across the river from Grand Tower, we would pass some time on the porch in rocking chairs and watch the river. I never knew any of the women in the Wilson family to ever have an idle hand—every one of them always carried a sewing basket with some kind of embroidery, lace making, or crocheting. They called it their "basket of work." Grandma was a great quilt maker and always embroidered her pieces with designs like the state birds or state flowers. At the end of the summer she would sit and snap green beans to prepare for canning while the other women worked from their baskets.

When I sat on the porch with my great-aunts, I always felt invisible, since their conversation never included me—it wasn't like today where a child is pretty much the center of attention at any gathering. I don't remember any of them ever asking me a question or for an opinion about anything. Sometimes, when they called me by my nickname "the orphan," my attention would be drawn back into their talk with a wave of humiliation and embarrassment. Then I'd remember that my life wasn't normal because I spent so much time staying at other people's houses. Mother and Daddy always said the island was too isolated for babysitters to stay there, but that didn't explain why we all weren't at home together.

I never knew why I was away from home so much. If anybody ever made me feel bad about it, Grandma sensed it and tried to make me feel better. She was quick to change the subject and sometimes said later that the other people in the family were just jealous because Grandpa Wilson liked me the most. But that never made me feel any better; having Grandpa Wilson like me wasn't much of a plus in my life. I dreaded "visiting" with him.

The day after I got there, Grandma said, "Go in and say hi to him," and I knew it was time to pay my respects. By then he was a frail, crusty old man who passed his time sitting in a rocking chair in the middle of the room—slowing rocking back and forth, just the same all day long.

He always faced the TV and a side window through which you could see over the field that stretched south to Tower Rock. He spent hours sitting there just staring, rocking, and twiddling his thumbs—first this way and then that.

I knew instinctively what to do—I sat down in another chair in the room and said, "Hi, Grandpa."

He kept rocking for a few minutes while he chewed on his "tabacci" and spit once or twice into the spittoon to his right. I just waited.

Finally, he asked, "How's your daddy doing? How's things down there on the island?"

"Fine," I answered.

Then he started talking in bits and pieces—probably it was the same way thoughts floated around in his mind.

Grandma used to say that the time her dad lived and worked on the island was the best time of his life, so it had to be talked about with me because that was where I lived. When he was a young man he got his start by working for my father's father, Mr. Cyrus F. Clark, who lived up in Audrain County, Missouri. It was an odd fact in my family that my great-grandfather Frank Wilson, my mother's grandfather, was born in 1872 while my grandfather on my father's side, Cyrus F. Clark, was born in 1847. In other words, my grandfather Clark was twenty-five years older than Great-Grandfather Wilson. Every time I visited he would tell me about how he used to work for Grandpa Clark on one of his farms up around Audrain County in what was known as the Wilson Township. It was first settled in 1821, and by 1850 there were a lot of Wilsons and Berrys living all around Goodwater Creek and Possum Walk Creek. Later they were laid to rest in Skull Lick Cemetery. Around 1915 Grandpa Wilson brought his family down to the island to farm it for Grandpa Clark.

"There's no better man that ever lived than your grandpa Clark—he was a good man to work for," he told me for the hundredth time. "I took my whole family down there onto that island—cleared

most of the land that's been cleared. We worked hard clearing that land without a tractor, you know. We did it with just a team."

His voice got louder as he talked, and he always seemed to be mad like he was stewing over something. It would be the most I would hear him talk all summer.

"I built that schoolhouse that your mother and daddy lived in after they were married. Now, your daddy came south in forty-six, didn't he? He floated a barge down the river with tools and such after the war. Your daddy built himself a new house since then, didn't he, after they put the levee in? Y'all don't live in the schoolhouse any more, do ya?"

"No," I said, thinking that the schoolhouse was long gone. I knew we'd lived in it for a few years, but I had no memory of the place. Now it was just a clearing on the other side of the yard that couldn't be plowed.

"I built that schoolhouse for all my own. Your grandma, there"—he nodded toward the kitchen where Grandma was working—"she taught school to her brothers before she hitched up with Wamp. Your grandpa, Mr. Cyrus F. Clark, he never set foot on the island, but a lot of men from up there in Mexico used to come down every year to go huntin'. They were a fine group of men from Audrain County. Your grandpa Clark, he owned a lot of farms up there and a bank too. Why, he was even a state senator. Did you know that?" He turned to look at me with a quick glaring stare but didn't wait for an

answer—his head was cocked to one side, and his eyes were squinted. I nodded and looked down until he went on.

"Well, don't ever forget that. You've got some fine blood in you, and it was a good day for the Wilsons when your mother married into the Clark family. Mr. Cyrus F. Clark, yes sirree Bob, he was just about the finest horse breeder in Missouri—in the whole country for that matter. Why those folks up in Mexico sold horses to the Queen of England and Buffalo Bill Cody, and your granddaddy was right there in the middle of it. President Roosevelt and McKinley, they all knew who he was, by God. He gave that Tom Bass his first job in the horse business. And your daddy's a good man too. Don't you ever let them tell ya any different. You know that, don't you?" He looked at me again, and I sensed that this time he wanted an answer.

I nodded and tried to remember why most of the Wilsons in Grand Tower didn't think too much of my daddy.

They never said anything to me and didn't have to—they showed how they felt with little shakes of their heads or by looking down to the ground at just the right time. My Wilson great-uncles didn't approve of my parents, but that didn't matter to their dad, Grandpa Wilson, since he idealized my dad's side of the family—the Clarks—and he was very happy when his granddaughter married one of them. Grandpa Wilson had lived in Mexico, Missouri, during the golden age of the Clarks, and he never forgot about all the horses that were sold to the most powerful men in the country out of Grandfather Clark's stable, and he knew about the thousands of acres of farms, the political connections, and the bank he once owned. Grandpa Wilson held on to the old-fashioned notion that powerful, rich men should be given respect for no other reason besides the fact that they had amassed money and power, plus he worked for Grandfather Clark all those years, so he grew to respect him firsthand. But his sons, the Wilson boys, had different opinions about the Clarks—I figured out later that they thought Daddy was spoiled, idealistic, drank too much, and was more than a little foolish. But maybe as Grandma said, "They were just jealous."

"How's the rest of your daddy's family? How's those two sisters of his? They're good women, but they should leave your daddy to it. From what I hear tell, they meddle too much!" All of a sudden, he was yelling. "What do they know about farming, being old maids and all?" I was glad he didn't wait for me to answer him that time. I didn't like my daddy's side of the family too much, and if I told him what I thought about them I knew he might get even madder than he was already—it wouldn't have helped anything.

"Now your grandpa Clark, he was a smart man—he didn't run out to join up during the War between the States. He knew better than that! Even at—what was he when the war started? Round about fourteen, I'd expect. He had more sense than my daddy's brothers. They would be your great-great-uncles—Daniel and James Scott Wilson. Have you heard tell of them?"

He looked around and glared at me again.

"Your uncle Daniel, he went with the Union. He was old enough, so they let him in. James Scott was too young, though, so they put him to work around the Union camps, but that wasn't good enough for him. No sirree Bob. He had other ideas! He wanted to see some o' the war." Grandpa Wilson started rocking faster and put his hands on the armrests of his chair like he was going to get up. I thought he might stand up too fast and fall over—then I'd have to jump up and catch him. Nothing could get people riled up faster than talk about the Civil War—but then he sank back in his chair again and put his hands on his lap. He overlapped his fingers a little to stop their shaking.

"Uncle Jim was fired up to go to war! He didn't know if he was comin' or goin'!" He started shaking his head and rocking at the same time. I watched him as he moved from side to side and back and forth all at once. Then he lifted his hand and waved it in front of his face and started talking in a high singsong type of voice that sounded like a girl's.

"So what do think he got in his mind to do? He ran off and joined up with some Confederate bushwhackers."

Then his voice went back to his normal bitter tone, and he stopped rocking his chair. "Daddy always said he was foolhardy. But you would have to say that his luck held out pretty good for him. If you're a reb and you're gonna get captured by Union militia, it's a good thing to have your own brother do the capturin', wouldn't you say?" He stopped rocking and leaned over to spit into the spittoon.

"Yes, Missy. I guess you could say that when Uncle Dan raided that cabin down there in southern Missoura and found his own brother holed up in it with a bunch of rebs—well that was Uncle Jim's lucky day." He started to rock again. "Uncle Dan let him walk in the back of the line, of the prisoners, you know, so he could slip into the woods. My own daddy had more sense than Uncle Jim; he was satisfied with hanging around the Union camps—he was only about twelve when it started up. Thank the good Lord he didn't join up with Johnny Reb, why we wouldn't be sitting here today if he had!" Grandpa Wilson stopped talking and rocking his chair—his eyes glazed over as he stared off into the distance toward Tower Rock. Grandma must have been listening from the kitchen for the right time to call out to me—I was done talking to Grandpa Wilson for the rest of the summer.

Four

A pilot, in those days, was the only unfettered and entirely independent human being that lived in the earth.

—Mark Twain

When you live alongside the Mississippi, the river isn't just water on the other side of the sandbar, it's more like something you feel close-up—like a big giant lying next to you in bed while you're sleeping—only it's still awake. There is a thread running through you that connects to other people who live up and down the river, and it's a powerful thing to have in common. Over the years we've learned from the histories of the people who went before us that the Mississippi can suddenly roll over into your life any time it wants to, so by necessity we're drawn together. Every day there is some kind of talk about the river; years of births, deaths, or any events that cause happiness or sorrow are marked by a mention of how high, low, or frozen it was at that particular time. In the winter the Mississippi freezes into chunks of ice and clogs up, during the spring the water floods into our homes, and in the fall it shrinks. Sandbars form one day and then disappear the next. High water causes debris to wash onto the land, but it usually floats away before we can figure out what it is. And then there are all the long hours we spend standing along the banks and watching the world go by like a kind of parade—but looking at the boats going up and down the river never made me feel left behind. Instead, there is a wonderful sense of being connected to the rest of the world—as if all of humankind is flowing past the front yard. The best times on Grandpa Wilson's farm were the peaceful moments spent in a rocking chair on the porch looking out at the "Missasip."

On the Wilson side they were farmers, but the Poe family—my mother's father's people—were all rivermen. My mother's great-grandfather, Livingston Poe, was the ferry keeper in Cape Girardeau in 1870. His people came mostly from North Carolina, through Kentucky and then to Missouri and Illinois. They were Swan, Elliot, Sumner, and Ford.

Livingston's son and my mother's grandfather, Charles Ferdinand Poe, was the captain of his own boat for most of his life. He drowned tragically in the river on the night of December 19, 1933, when he left the pilothouse of the steamer, *Kaskaskia,* to help the captain of the *Fort Chartes.* The two boats were tied together and were heading upriver just south of our island. The family always said he was "walking a moonbeam"—meaning that he mistook the reflection of the moon for a plank between the barges. He put his foot down on what he thought was the plank and then slipped into the river. When you walked a moonbeam, you thought you were on something solid and going someplace, but I guess you weren't doing either unless you counted the fact that he was going to his watery grave. His death was a great trauma for the Poe family coming as it did at the beginning of the Depression. It's easy to imagine how horrible falling in the river would have been for him, splashing down into the cold water, all the while knowing that he alone had made the mistake that would kill him. He left behind ten children—most of them girls, plus his wife and his mother-in-law, Ma Sumner, who was a fixture in the town and liked to entertain people with stories about running from the Yankees in Louisiana during the Civil War. The Poe family was a fun and boisterous group with almost as many daughters as the Wilsons had sons—they all had colorful nicknames like Weggie, Wamp, Ernie, and Blackie. My grandmother, Lola Wilson, married Wamp Poe, and her brother, Stacy Wilson, married Wamp's sister, Ernie Poe. It was always a joke in the family that a boy named Stacy married a girl named Ernie. During the early part of the twentieth century, the Poes lived in a shotgun house behind the Baptist Church in Grand Tower. Four generations are now buried in the Walker Hill Cemetery above the town.

Captain Charles F. Poe on the left, drowned December 19, 1933

Born by the River

My mother's father was also a riverboat captain—Wamp Poe was the pilot of the boat that took the first American satellite down the river to Cape Canaveral in 1958. He was also one of the few men still licensed to pilot a paddle-wheel steamboat in the 1960s. For most of his life he worked the typical riverman's schedule with a few months on and a few months off. He and my grandmother, Lola, had eight children, but only four of them lived—their family suffered tragedy beyond comprehension when two children died in the same week—one from polio and the other from whooping cough. The youngest of their four children was the famous riverman, Edgar Allen Poe—he was the pilot of the *General Jackson* for many years and became a colorful television personality in Nashville.

Around the time Uncle Eddie was born, my grandparents' marriage started to fall apart because my grandfather had started seeing his oldest daughter's best friend—in the end they ran off together and got married. By 1938 my grandmother, my mother, and Uncle Eddie were left on their own and had to move back to Grand Tower from Cape Girardeau where they had been living. Grandpa Poe and "Aunt Dessie," as we called her, ended up getting married and living out their lives together in Cape Girardeau. I always wondered whether or not Grandma was ever on the front porch of the Wilson farm and watching the river when her ex-husband passed by on a towboat—it must have happened more than once. He may have even looked over and seen her sitting there on the porch. I do remember one time when her son, my Uncle Eddie, was piloting down the river and saw her standing on a ladder cleaning windows. He called out on his horn, "Get down from that ladder, Mom, before you fall and break your neck!" She had fun with that one for years—she said she was so startled she almost fell off the ladder. Uncle Eddie was a fourth generation Mississippi River boat captain in the Poe family and that is a noble profession in those parts. As Mark Twain wrote, "When I was a boy, there was but one permanent ambition among my comrades in our village on the west bank of the Mississippi River. That was to be a steamboatman." Pilots are proud people because it's part of their job to have a lot of confidence in their own judgment. Uncle Eddie used to say that 90 percent of the job was just common sense.

Whenever I left the farm at the end of each summer, I didn't know enough to realize that during the winter my grandmother would spend weeks alone there without seeing another soul except for Grandpa Wilson. All through her sixties and into her seventies, she would have to get up in the dark and trudge through the snow to milk the cow and take care of livestock—and then do it all over again in the evening. I never thought to ask her why she didn't come to our house for Thanksgiving or why we never visited or called her during the winter. I could tell her heart was broken because I felt, even from a young age, that something was wrong. It was sad to think that her husband had deserted her at a time and in a place where that seldom happened, and then she had to give up everything to take care of her widowed father. My heart still goes out to her.

I'll always remember a cousin my age who came to the farm one time for a visit. Grandma saw the girl and her mom drive up to the house, and then she took me aside to say that life had been hard for them so I needed to be extra nice. When they came in I stood at attention the way we always did when a grown-up entered the room. Right away you could tell there was a kind of formal and nervous air about them. The daughter sat down on the edge of one of the rocking chairs with her toes just touching the floor—her long graceful hands lay crossed on her lap. My grandmother and her mother visited in a kindly way, but my cousin seemed distant and frozen—her stiff jaw held tight, and she seemed determined to stay hidden behind her wing-tipped glasses. I was a little relieved when she turned down a chance to go outside with me—her dress with its cancan skirt and bolero jacket wouldn't have held up very well beyond the porch.

I remember sitting and staring at her while I rocked my chair back and forth, waiting to see what we would do. There were a few girls in my school who always wore dresses and managed to stick together with their tidy hairdos held down by barrettes or bows, and she reminded me of them. It was puzzling, though, because nobody ever told me to be extra nice to them—the girls at school who looked like her seemed to be doing just fine. Eventually I began to notice she was looking at my tennis shoes and that her eyes were gradually rising over my shorts and striped T-shirt. I looked down to see what she was looking at and noticed how ragged and dirty I was. Our eyes soon locked in a stare down that she broke first when she tilted her head upward to glance away. My heart sank as I realized she felt a cut above me. Once again, I was having that old familiar feeling of being confused by what the grown-ups told me about the world and the reality of what I saw for myself. After all she was supposed to be having a harder time in life than I was. Her mother, on the other hand, seemed a little nervous and shy, as if she was there for a reason and hadn't gotten around to it yet. She gently nudged her daughter to go outside with me.

"Do you want to see the chickens?" I asked her for the second time. Like always, I was anxious to get out of the stifling house, but I knew it wouldn't be right for me to go off rambling by myself and leave her there. She was our guest, so that meant I had official obligations; I was well trained by both sides of my family on those kinds of responsibilities. For everybody from around those parts, guests came first no matter what the situation—being hospitable was one of the most important rules we were taught, and there were no questions to be asked about it.

She drew back in her chair and looked at her mother— she'd already said "no" to me once. I stood up and waited.

Born by the River

Her mother asked, "Of course, you would like to see the chickens wouldn't you, honey?" My cousin's confidence seemed to fade as we made our way down the porch and over to the chicken coop—she dragged behind me, carefully watching her step. I slowed down and pointed out a puddle to her—I was never able to hold a grudge against anyone who thought they were better than me. Part of me knew I deserved it since I was the "orphan." But I also knew enough to recognize that whoever was in control of the situation at hand was not inferior to the other person, and since I was in control of the chicken coop I could afford to be nice to her. Because of the odd circumstances in my life, I often bounced between extremes of confidence and insecurity, and I learned early on that I needed to be able to adjust the dial on both. Overconfidence put you at risk for foolishness, and insecurity was blood in the water to anyone who might want to take you down. On the other hand, my cousin was somewhere in the middle because she knew what she was about—it was easy for her to find her step through the barnyard by picking out the high ground. It seemed like she had something in spades that I was missing—she knew very well who she was and where she stood in the world. I never found out what they came for, but when they left that afternoon, her clothes were clean and her barrettes were still in place.

Five

*It is self-evident that Saint Louis affected me
more deeply than any other environment has ever
done. I feel that there is something in having
passed one's childhood beside the big river, which
is incommunicable to those people who have not.*

—T. S. Eliot

At the end of that summer Daddy came to pick me up at
Grandma's. Usually after Labor Day I would cross the
river with Uncle Price and go back to school, but this year
was different—at the time, I didn't know why.

*It seemed funny to see Daddy carrying a little suitcase when he
came into the house on that hot morning in August. He barely said
"boo" to any of us before he sank into a rocking chair—then he just
stared off into space for what seemed like the longest time. We could all
tell that something big was bothering him. Grandma stood off to the
side of the front room near the kitchen with her hands clasped together*

at her waist and a troubled look on her face. Grandpa Wilson stopped rocking in his chair and made a grumpy sound; then he leaned over and spat into his spittoon. I took a seat in another rocker—my eyes drifted out the window where a towboat was heading downstream. It wasn't unusual for us to sit and not say anything to each other like that, but there was a knot in my stomach that tightened up.

After a while Daddy nodded toward the suitcase and told me to go change my clothes. When I took the little bag up to Grandma's room and opened it, my heart sank at the sight of dresses inside. I knew what was coming. I pulled out a dress and put it on, all the time shuddering at the thought of the behavior and the place that went along with wearing it.

The plan was that we were going to drive up to Saint Louis where I would catch the train by myself to Kansas City. Aunt Liz, his middle sister, would pick me up at the train station, and then I'd be staying with her for a whole week. At that time in my life there was nothing more terrible for me than to go to Topeka, Kansas, and stay with my Aunt Liz. Especially horrible was the thought that I'd have to leave one of my favorite places—the farm where my grandmother lived— and go off to the most hateful place in the world. I knew very well what that week would be like—Aunt Liz was a deliberate, controlling old maid, and I'd be forced to sit still and mind my manners until I would bust.

Both my dad's sisters never married, so they spent long hours drilling me on my manners and schooling me on important things. All this involved a lot of work—there would be more than one museum to go to and many hours spent looking into dusty glass cases; then Aunt Liz would ask me about what we'd seen and maybe even make me write something down. In the yard, she would tell me the names of plants and birds and talk endlessly about the Audubon Society and things like how starlings weren't native to America. In the house, I would have to listen to all kinds of lectures about silver, linen, and furniture and how to take care of them. With so much training and so little time, she had her work cut out for her—plus she needed to make up for the bad influences and wild upbringing that were destroying me when I wasn't in her care. I can't remember her ever criticizing my mother's side of the family, but she had a way of making it clear that there was no end to the mess I was in because of them. She was unlike anybody I knew or have ever known since, and most of the time I intensely disliked being with her.

And so I complained constantly during the two-hour drive north into Saint Louis. Daddy tried to calm me down and told me that I had to be nice to Aunt Liz.

As he tried to fill the role of being a parent, he always fell into the same lecture—I should respect my elders no matter what they said or did, I should never cuss, and I should never smoke cigarettes. Nothing was worse than a woman smoking a cigarette and cussing. For some reason, he thought that those three things—smoking, cussing, and respecting my elders—were all I needed to know about steering through life. I guess he thought that by respecting my elders I would be obeying all the rules and that by not swearing and smoking, I'd be behaving in a ladylike manner. And if he'd been drinking, he would add that I should try to marry someone with the last name of Clark so I could carry on the family name. I walked away from those conversations knowing that my dad had some very important expectations about my behavior and always felt his sway over me as I went through life. In other words, by generalizing the rules he succeeded in making me fit them to everything.

Looking out the window I watched the hills and farms pass slowly by us while we bounced along in Daddy's old Ford pickup truck. Fields gradually turned into towns and country roads into busy highways at a pace that let me adjust to the change that Saint Louis would bring. Even with the windows down there was no relief from the humid August morning, and the air only became more stifling as we drove into the city. As usual, we headed straight to the University City neighborhood where Daddy's cousin, Eleanor, lived.

A farm in southern Missouri and an affluent neighborhood in Saint Louis are two very different worlds located less than a hundred miles from each other. But I learned from a young age how to navigate through them—the adjustments were quick and came naturally to me. Not everything was different, though—some of the rules were the same, like respecting your elders and taking care of company. The main thing I didn't like about Daddy's side was that it was harder to get away to be by yourself around the Clark family. It seemed like somebody was always keeping track of me, and there was never a chance for a ramble when I was around them.

By the early 1960s there weren't any Roths left in the downtown area of the city where my great-grandfather, Adam Roth, had started his grocery supply business and raised his family. I'd been given tours to those parts over the years when we drove down Twenty-Third Street and saw where their early house used to be. Then there was the big house with its twenty-two rooms at 3201 Locust Street and a complete tour with Aunt Liz would have included a drive around where the early stores used to be at the corner of Fifth and Spruce. After quickly passing by those places, she would take me to the main home office of the Roth grocery supply business at 435 South Seventh Street, which is now a parking lot for Busch Stadium. The Roth family had lived in the downtown area of Saint Louis for over a hundred years, but I always felt a little puzzled about why we were driving through that part of the city. Everybody acted like it was so important, but there was nothing left to look at—the houses had been long since torn down, and the stores had become abandoned buildings.

Adam Roth was Daddy's grandfather. He'd come to America from Germany with his family in 1836 when he was ten years old. By the time he died in 1900 he was known as the "Merchant Prince" of Saint Louis, and his wholesale grocery company was supplying just about every grocery store from Colorado to Ohio and from Texas to Minnesota. He'd started his business in a log cabin at the northwest corner of Fifth (now Broadway) and Spruce Streets with a few dry goods and a lot of big ambitions. The Roths had landed in Baltimore in 1836 and then traveled by stagecoach to Pittsburgh; after that, they came down the Ohio River and then up the Mississippi River to the Saint Louis area, where they bought a farm on the Illinois side.

When he was fourteen, Adam crossed the river on the ferry and rode into Saint Louis with his father on a wagon loaded with produce to sell at the Old Soulard Market. After a few trips to town, a doctor offered him a job and a place to sleep, so he ended up moving into the growing metropolis. Before his father left, though, he made sure Adam was enrolled in school during the evenings—he didn't want him running wild on the Saint Louis waterfront every night. My great-grandfather finished school at eighteen and then took a job for eight dollars a month on one of the steamboats that was docked down on the river bank. Plying the Mississippi, the boat stopped at small towns along the river where Adam got to know the local grocers. By the time he was twenty-two, Adam was back in Saint Louis with his head full of new ideas and a little money in his pocket—he had his hopes set on buying out his brother-in-law's sixteen-by-thirty-foot drygoods store. In 1849 he paid $150 for the little log cabin on the corner, but his first year in business would turn out to be one of the worst in Saint Louis history.

Adam Roth's first store, 1849

During that time Saint Louis was truly the gateway to the West. People were flooding into town on their way to the California Gold Rush, and the city was bursting at the seams. The booming population was too much for the city to handle; a cholera epidemic broke out that ended up killing 10 percent of the population—almost five thousand people. Then on May 17, 1849, a paddle-wheeled steamboat called *The White Cloud* caught fire at its moorings on the end of Cherry Street. Before the fire was out, the boat was adrift on the river where it spread the inferno to over twenty-two other steamboats. Several other barges and flatboats also went up in flames. Eleven hours later, the fire was contained, but three people were dead, and fifteen square blocks of Saint Louis were destroyed. The fire wiped out 430 buildings, but the Adam Roth Grocery Store survived.

For the next few years, while the city struggled to rebuild, Adam sold groceries in the front of the store during the day and slept on a cot in the back at night. The postfire building codes called for all the new structures to be made of either stone or brick, and water and sewage systems were put into place. In 1849 Saint Louis had a population of only about sixty thousand, but the town was growing wildly. Soon it would be the second-largest port in the United States, and after the railroads came to town, the population tripled. In just a few years it changed from a small landing for the French fur trade to the largest city west of Pittsburgh. Adam soon expanded his business to delivering groceries around town—he was in the right place at the right time since he was living in a city that was coming of age the same time he was. With his business thriving and a clerk on hand to help him out in the store, his thoughts turned to settling down. One evening he and his younger brother, Ben, were invited to a party at the home of another German family. It was there that the two brothers fell in love with two sisters, Margaretha and Mary Arnold. The four of them married in a double wedding on August 8, 1854.

Margaretha and Mary Arnold's parents, Jacob Arnold and Catherine Becker Arnold, were also German immigrants. They met while they were making the crossing from Europe to New Orleans in 1832, four years before Adam's family had arrived. After Catherine's mother died in Germany, her father decided to bring his five children to America. But during the transatlantic voyage, he became sick with cholera and died. Catherine Becker and her four siblings were shocked and desolate as they stood on the deck of the ship and watched their father's body slide off the boat and into the sea. Jacob Arnold was watching as well and couldn't help but fall in love with the young girl who was so vulnerable and grief-stricken. Catherine, the oldest of the five, was nineteen years old when she landed in New Orleans in 1832. Aunt Liz always treasured a pewter plate that Catherine Becker brought with her to America on her miserable journey. In New Orleans, Catherine bravely followed the plans laid out by her father and managed to obtain passage to Saint Louis for herself and her siblings. Once onboard the boat, while she traveled north on the Mississippi, she reconnected with Jacob Arnold—the young man who'd helped her get through the trying time of her father's death on the ship coming over from Germany. Eighteen months later they were married in a Lutheran church in Saint Louis.

At the time of their wedding, in 1834, Saint Louis was a small village with a population of only seven thousand. French trappers claimed the land from the Osage Indians in 1764. Along with their African slaves, the trappers built the town as a landing for shipping furs from the territories out west to downriver in New Orleans. The early French families lived in masonry homes, while pioneers settled in log cabins; the center of life was on the riverfront. The western boundary of the city was Fourth Street, and beyond that was pure wilderness for the next two thousand miles. My great-great-grandfather, Jacob Arnold, was a blacksmith and was famous for making wagons that held up well for pioneers who were heading out west from Saint Louis. He had a reputation for quality work, and many settlers wouldn't begin their journeys across the continent until he had inspected their wagons.

Things changed for Jacob Arnold, though, in 1849 when gold was discovered in California, and he started helping the forty-niners outfit themselves for the gold rush. Watching others follow their dreams became harder and harder for Jacob, and by 1850 he'd heard enough stories about miners plucking gold nuggets out of streams and getting rich quick. Like so many others, he was struck with gold fever and left for California along with 150,000 men and women who crossed the continent overland during those times. Another 150,000 would travel by ship. Catherine supported his decision and helped him prepare for the journey by packing up his gear and carefully sewing money into the lining of his clothes. He left her in Saint Louis with six children, including my great-grandmother, Margaretha, who was twelve at the time. He was gone for fourteen months until he became disillusioned with life out west—his dreams of gold were shattered. When he came home, he was shaken up by what he'd seen and quickly reassured Catherine and the children that he was home to stay. Jacob was happy to go back to making wagons at the edge of civilization and worked until he died in 1863 at the age of fifty-two. At the time of his death, the Civil War had been raging for two years, and his daughter, Margaretha Arnold, was twenty-six years old. She had been married to Adam Roth for nine years.

During the Civil War, Missouri was one of the most divided states in the Union, but Saint Louis was forced to pick a side. Not only was Missouri a border state, but along with Kentucky, it was one of only two states with an active dual government represented in both Washington, DC, and Richmond, Virginia. As the rumblings for war began, Missourians realized there would be no easy escape from the destruction it would bring to a state so torn. In a futile shot at avoiding the struggles, they came up with an impossible plan—they would stay with the Union but remain neutral. The idea was that they would not give supplies or soldiers to either side and would fight any troops who entered the state. It was a complicated plan that was doomed from the beginning, and by the time the war ended, Missouri had supplied roughly 110,000 troops to the Union and 40,000 troops to the Confederacy.

The war first hit home on May 10, 1861, when a battle over the Saint Louis arsenal broke out that left twenty people dead on the streets. Missouri Governor Claiborne Fox Jackson was for the South; he quickly marked off a site for a military camp in Saint Louis and started to make plans for Missouri to secede from the Union. When the lines were drawn, Adam Roth's brother, Henry, helped organize a home guard regiment to hold Saint Louis to the Union. Within a week of my great-grandfather, Adam, joining up with the Third United States Reserve Corp of the Missouri Volunteers, more than one hundred and fifty customers closed their accounts at his grocery store.

After "Camp Jackson" was seized by a regiment loyal to the Union, violence became a nightly occurrence in the city. Adam spent many nights guarding the railroad depots and supply dumps, while his wife, Margaretha, remained home alone with their three children. For safety reasons, he told them to stay in the same room and sleep on the floor. At the time, Margaretha was seven months pregnant with their fourth child, Richard Jacob—he would survive for only thirteen months in the tumultuous time. In August 1861, martial law was declared, and order was restored to the city. After things settled down in Saint Louis, Adam returned to work and gave open credit to all Union soldiers—he marked many accounts "payable when the war is over." He also extended credit to all the confederate soldiers he knew personally. By the time the war was over, one thousand dollars had been loaned to the families of veterans.

Four years later my father's mother, Sophia Margaretha Roth, was born in 1869. Because most Missourians had gone with the Union, the state managed to avoid the military occupations and reconstruction that devastated so much of the South after the war. Lincoln Republicans kept their power in Missouri until 1873 when Democrats, led by ex-Confederate soldiers, returned to power. After the Democrats regained control, Jim Crow laws took hold in the state, and ex-confederate soldiers like Jesse James became folk heroes—he was also known as "the last confederate soldier."

The 1870s was a roller-coaster time for the city since the devastation from the war continued. When the panic of 1873 hit the local economy, times were tough; however, civic leaders pulled off a big win for Saint Louis in 1876 when the city hosted the Democratic convention where they nominated Samuel Tilden for president. Tilden would go on to win the election with a vote of 4,285,992 to Hayes's 4,033,768 in one of the most contentious elections in US history. Tilden was awarded 184 electoral votes and Hayes 165, but twenty electoral votes were under dispute in four states. In the end, a deal was made that would see Hayes get the twenty electoral votes if the Republicans agreed to end Reconstruction—federal troops would be withdrawn from the South, and the Democratic Redeemers would once again be in control of the old Confederacy. It was called the Compromise of 1877—my grandmother, Sophie, was eight years old when Rutherford B. Hayes was awarded the presidency in this back-room deal.

Six

*We are strange beings, we seem to go free, but
we go in chains—chains of training, custom,
convention, association, environment—in
a word, circumstance—and against these
bonds the strongest of us struggle in vain.*

—MARK TWAIN

My father always made sure I was up on my family history whenever we visited his people—I guess that was part of his attitude about respecting your elders. His first cousin, Eleanor, lived in the University City neighborhood of Saint Louis in a beautiful brick house full of antiques and oriental rugs; it had three stories and five bathrooms and was the most beautiful home I'd ever seen. The family ended up selling it to Edward Erker, the head brewmaster for Anheuser-Busch. It became notorious when he was murdered in his bed only two weeks after he moved into the house.

When I went there with Mother, she wouldn't dare go into the house in pants or shorts. She always kept a wrap skirt under the seat of her car, and after she parked she would whip it out and tie it on. But my dad always just pulled up in his pickup truck dressed straight from the farm without a thought about how he looked. Nobody could pass from country farmer to high-toned city dweller as easily as he did—he always had a way of making you think that every human being should be treated with respect, no matter who they were.

When I was about seven, one of the most exciting moments of my life happened at Cousin Eleanor's house when Little Ellie, Cousin Eleanor's oldest daughter, married into a well-born family from Philadelphia. Mother's eyes always lit up when she talked about how they'd met on a ship coming from London to New York. She said it was the most romantic way two people could ever meet. Of course, Aunt Liz made sure she picked out my dress for the wedding and added all kinds of instructions when she gave it to me. Mother said that Aunt Liz didn't trust her to buy our clothes for such a crucial event. After the dress came the training about how to behave on the big day—in the months before the wedding, I felt as if the whole world might slip away and disintegrate if I didn't behave perfectly. I was terrified all the way up to the wedding and was completely miserable at the thought of it.

I understood the high stakes that were playing out later on in life when it came out that Daddy's cousin Eleanor was really the one who didn't like to behave. She had a reputation for being pretty wild. I found out about her younger years when we were together around the time the King Tut exhibit came to America. Somebody asked her if she was planning on seeing it; she made a face and said she already had. That seemed unlikely since the exhibit had never been to America, but then she went on to say that she'd been to Egypt in 1925 and had seen it there. Mother told me that her parents had sent her on a long trip to Europe and Egypt when she first took up with the man who was to be her future husband; he was not thought to be somebody she should marry because his family was from the wrong side of town. Unfortunately for her she came back and married him anyway.

We all lived by the same rules—they weren't written down or spoken, but that only made them more commanding. We were under their yoke whether we were in Grand Tower or Saint Louis. Cousin Eleanor shattered the most important social commandments of our world when she got married to the man from the other side of the tracks. Everybody knew what class they were in, and we knew that whenever the laws were broken, things would fall apart. In order to keep up the boundaries between the social classes, children were constantly being reminded of people who had ignored the rules or made mistakes. We were told you would pay a big price in the end if you disobeyed them and that you could never be happy marrying anybody beneath you. Your family would also suffer, and you'd bring shame to everyone.

At the top of the heap were the families who were called "very good," next were "good" families, then came the "common" people, and at the bottom were the "trash" (the word "trash" was never officially said out loud). Everybody claimed that the system was not based on money or education but on who your relations were. This was usually true, but people with money could move up if they behaved themselves. Mostly, though, you could never change from one slot to the other, even by marriage. A credit to the system was that children were supposed to respect all people equally no matter what spot they held—we were trained to never be rude. In the end you weren't supposed to feel like you were better than others, only that there were certain things you couldn't do with them—like fall in love and get married.

So when Cousin Eleanor came back from her exile in Europe and married beneath her, she kept her status—but her husband's didn't change any. Their poor children's fate would be up in the air and dependent on how the family lived. If they had enough money and continued in the same manner as their mother's family—which is usually what happened, since the women in the family set the tone of the household—they would still be "very good." But if they slipped up there would be problems—they would have to be careful about who they ran with. Of course, the status of her children would remain the same within the family. No one ever betrayed a family member because of what they did or who they married; you'd just feel sorry for them because you knew things would go bad soon enough. The saying was, "Low origin will make itself known."

When Eleanor's daughter, Little Ellie, married into the high-toned family from Philadelphia she insured her place at the top, and that helped to elevate the whole family. All this was probably the main reason why I had to behave myself at her wedding. The lower status of Little Ellie's dad meant their branch of the family was on the edge of a precipice. This shaky spot was magnified by the extra-high status of the Philadelphia mainliners she was marrying into. As "outsiders" they couldn't be classified within any of our categories, but we all knew they were at the top of the heap in their own part of the country, so their status was secure.

Cousin Eleanor may have been able to marry her daughter off to a prominent family, but in the end her own life didn't turn out so well. While "very good" families could marry into "good" families—that was fine—"good" families could not hitch themselves to common people or trash. Those marriages were doomed from the start, and they would only end in misery—which is exactly what happened to Cousin Eleanor.

The inside of Cousin Eleanor's house felt like thick humid air when you come up from a cave on a hot day—it hit you. The smell of the citrus oil caking on polished walnut drifted through the dark rooms, and there was a sense that somebody was watching from the shadows—watching to make sure you minded your manners. I'd left the land of the Wilsons and was now in the dominion of the Roths. In her house, my first instinct was to sit down and stay still, which was just what everybody expected me to do; after an hour or so, if I was lucky, the housekeeper might come in and take me into the kitchen for a drink of water. As usual, I was to be seen and not heard. The adults would rarely say "boo" to me, so my only option was to stay put and try following the talk of the grown-ups while I looked around the room. If we weren't in one of the public rooms of the house, there were photographs around, and by that time I could make out pictures of my grandmother. There was one I remember of her with her two sisters—they were all dressed up as debutants for the Veiled Prophet Ball (or the "VP Ball" as they called it). In the black-and-white photo, it looked like she was in a beautiful white dress. You would think she was getting married if you hadn't known any better.

I never met my grandmother, so I didn't have a name for her like "Grandma" or "Nana"—for me her name was always Sophie Margaretha Roth Clark. She was the eighth child in the family when she was born in 1869 (there would be four more girls for a total of eleven children who lived past infancy). Her parents, Adam Roth and Margaretha Arnold Roth, were only one generation removed from the old country, so they held to German traditions. Their home was known for its harmonious atmosphere. In 1869 her dad, Adam, owned a booming grocery supply company, but his expansion to selling only wholesale wouldn't happen for another six years. The Civil War had ended four years before her birth, and Saint Louis, like the rest of the country, was still recovering from the tragedy. While she was a toddler, a downturn in the economy called the Panic of 1873 devastated most of the businesses in the area. But her father worked hard to make sure his company survived. Just like during the cholera epidemic, the Great Fire, and the Civil War—people still had to eat. Adam Roth managed things very well, and by 1875 he had moved his offices to a four-story building at 109 North Main Street. In 1885 the business was incorporated, and his two oldest sons were his partners. Around the time Sophie turned twenty-one, he moved operations to yet another larger location with warehouses and railroad shipping facilities located in the same building. Railroad cars were loaded directly from the platform at the rear of the business and shipped to their destination without handling them again. Thousands of retail merchants across America bought products marked with the Roth's trademark: Early Breakfast coffee and Squirrel Brand canned goods. In another big move around 1890, the family built a new twenty-three room home at 3201 Locust Street. It was a grand house where they lived for the next seventeen years.

Roth house at 3201 Locust Street, circa 1890

Born by the River

Sophie came of age in a large, prosperous family that was enjoying life the same way so many other wealthy Victorian families were across the country—they embraced a reserved social scene of receptions, balls, and charities while accumulating wealth and proudly showing it off. They balanced affluence with church work and an active social life with conservative reserve. The women of the family were educated at Lindenwood College, the first college for women west of the Mississippi, while the men were groomed for the family business. The girls gave one another engraved opera glasses and gold thimbles as they accumulated silver and linens for trousseaus, but in the end, out of seven daughters only two would marry—Sophie and Beulah, the youngest of the family. After she graduated from Lindenwood College, Sophie returned home around the time her father was turning the business over to his sons—Adam was retiring, and he and his wife wanted to travel. Sophie joined the family on trips to Mexico, Alaska, and California. Her father died in 1900 at the age of seventy-three, and her mother, Margaretha, died two years later. Sophie was thirty-three when her mother was buried, and she wouldn't marry for four more years. Adam and Margaretha Arnold Roth raised ten children to adulthood, but out of the ten only five married; in the end, they would have twelve children and fourteen grandchildren.

The Roth family in 1883; Sophia Margaretha Roth, second from left; Adam and Margaretha Arnold Roth, seated at the table

Sophia Margaretha Roth
Christmas 1893, dressed for the Veiled Prophet Ball

Seven

Doesn't make any difference who we are or what
we are, there's always somebody to look down on.

—MARK TWAIN

*I*t felt good to have a break between Cousin Eleanor and Aunt
Liz, so by the time Daddy dropped me off at the depot I was
happy to be on the train by myself. As it pulled out of the station
in Saint Louis, I found an aisle seat by a well-dressed teenage girl.
It was a relief to have a spot next to somebody close to my own age,
and I thought we might talk to each other while we had a fun ride to
Kansas City. The train felt familiar and exciting to me because of all
the hours I'd passed on Grandpa Wilson's porch watching the passengers' profiles fly by in a blur while they headed north to Saint Louis
or south to Memphis. Now it was my turn to be inside that world.
At first I didn't have the nerve to try to talk to the girl next to me
since she was older than I was and seemed a little sophisticated. So I
waited patiently while she stared out the window. We both watched as
the rough edges of the city went slowly by us, with me looking more at

her back than at the scenery. Gradually a feeling of disappointment and rejection passed over me while I tried to remember how far it was to Kansas City—it would be a long way, and there was nothing to do but sit. Why couldn't she at least acknowledge me, I wondered—after all, we were even dressed alike; it was a good thing I had that dress on after all. Then I started to feel a little hungry and remembered how Daddy had given me some money for lunch and pointed out the dining car in the next compartment forward. Right then, a brilliant idea dawned on me: she was wearing a watch, so I could ask her the time. It would start us off on the right foot in a casual but friendly kind of way, and then we would get to know each other.

But when I said, "Excuse me, do you know what time it is," she continued to ignore me.

I asked her again, but she kept her head turned toward the window. Then my feelings of disappointment and rejection changed pretty quickly to anger. I was filling up with irritation and started to think about confronting her—it was hard to believe anybody could be so rude. I was being scorned, and it felt shameful to me—I couldn't help but wonder what it was about me that was so repulsive to her. What was so bad that this girl couldn't even answer a simple question? That old familiar feeling of not really belonging was sweeping over me again.

Then the conductor came by to check our tickets. Even though he was talking directly to her, she still kept looking out the window. Finally, he leaned over me and waved his hand in front of her face. It was then that it dawned on me—she couldn't hear. She was startled a little but quickly found her ticket and handed it to him while I sank back into my seat. I was flabbergasted. The first thing that came to mind was how close I'd come to behaving rudely to her. Then a great feeling of relief swept over me when I realized how embarrassing it would've been—I'd come within an inch of asking her why she was so mean. The truth was, she wasn't being an unkind person at all because not only could she not hear, but she knew we wouldn't be able to talk to each other anyway. It took me a minute to compose myself and think about everything that was going on. I turned to look around the car to see if anybody else was looking at us. Had the other passengers known what I was thinking? Had they seen me getting angry? More relief passed over me when it seemed like nobody was looking at us— everybody was just going about their own business in the usual way. By now the conductor was gone, and she was staring out the window again—all this had happened so quickly, and things were back to exactly where they were before the porter had checked our tickets.

There weren't any deaf people in Grand Tower, but there was a man in our town who couldn't speak, so I understood that everything else about her would be the same as any other teenage girl. Coming from a small town like Grand Tower, we didn't grow up knowing about all the different types of people in the world. But we did learn that if they were in our town, they should be accepted by the community. For the most part, the people in the town were all just made of different ingredients of the same living thing.

Born by the River

The situation swirled around in my head while I sat there trying to digest what had happened, but it was hard to figure out because there were just too many new things going on at the same time.

Almost all of my experiences, up to that point, were of people and things that had been there from my birth—before I had words for them. New events didn't happen very often, and on the train that day, there weren't any grown-ups around to sort it all out.

For the third time in the course of fifteen minutes my opinion of her had changed—I'd gone from thinking about her as someone who might be a friend to deciding she was a really mean person and then realizing she couldn't hear or talk. It was obvious we wouldn't be able have a conversation, but the desire to connect with her was still in me. I glanced over at her again and reconsidered everything I knew about this stranger on the train. Then I impulsively put my hand on her arm. She turned and smiled at me as I pointed to my wrist and asked her what time it was. She looked directly at my mouth and then held up her watch and showed me the time. Thank goodness we had finally made some contact with each other. I looked at her watch and saw it was one forty-five.

"Thank you," I said. It was past lunchtime, and that was a good excuse to pick up my purse and walk toward the dining car. I felt more than a little shaken up and was ready to move on to something else.

In my family, we would have called the porter who helped me get my suitcase onto the train a "colored man." I'd heard the word "negro" before, but it wasn't used much around Grand Tower. I learned how to think about black people from the adults around me without situations or words I can recall. When you pick up ideas that way you grow up feeling like they are facts, not opinions, and you keep thinking that way until somebody tells you something different.

Mostly I heard about the blacks who used to live in town when people mentioned the places of their past. Somebody would say, "They live next door to the old colored schoolhouse" or "His car broke down behind the old colored Baptist Church." But by the time I was born, those places were just piles of rubble, and the only blacks left in Grand Tower were old folks. They lived in run-down houses that were scattered around those same old landmarks like the dilapidated schoolhouse. There was an old couple who owned a piece of land around Front Street, but it was said that it was silly for them to buy it.

"Why would you buy land where you couldn't live?" people would ask with a shake of their heads. But the townspeople didn't answer those questions, so I never figured out why they couldn't live on Front Street.

Then there was the old man who had the same last name as ours. One time he walked the two and a half miles down to the island to bring us a piece of mail he'd gotten by mistake when it was delivered to his post office box in Grand Tower. Daddy was shocked to see him lumbering down the levee road. I remember standing in the front yard and listening while Daddy thanked him about a million times for bringing us the mail. Then he explained to the old man that he didn't need to walk all the way down to the island to deliver our mail and that the next time he should just give it back to the man at the post office. All the postman had to do was put it into our box, and then we would pick it up.

He was a sickly-looking old colored man, and I couldn't imagine how he ever walked the two and a half miles from Grand Tower down to our house. We got him something to drink and eat, and then the three of us piled into Daddy's truck, with me sitting in the middle, and drove him back to his home in town. I watched while Daddy walked him up to his porch; then Daddy reached into his pocket and handed him something. Of course, all the way home I got the lecture about how we should always be respectful to older people, especially colored folks.

"Did I ever tell you about John?" he asked me for what seemed like the millionth time. I already knew Daddy was going to ask me if I'd ever heard about the man who worked for his family for so long. I could tell because he was talking to the old, colored man in the same kind of voice he always used when he talked about John. John Logan was a man who'd worked for them for years. He was born in slavery in

November of 1847, the same month and year that my grandfather, Cyrus F. Clark, was born. It was always an odd thing for me to think about—those two lives that were so important to my dad both being born at the same time yet under such different circumstances. Then I skipped right to the good part of John's story, something I'd heard Mother say.

"Did you love John more than your own daddy?" He waited for a long time before he spoke, and then he said, "They say I did."

"You must have been sad when he died."

My father didn't speak, so I was miserable to think that a question I already knew the answer to had put an end to the talk we were having—it was the part of the story Daddy didn't like. As we rode along on the levee road I started to feel bad about reminding him of John's dying—now we had to mark a quiet time of respect for the dead instead of talking.

It was never said outright, but I knew we were supposed to feel like we were better than the old, colored man we'd just dropped off. And although Daddy loved John, I knew he felt like he was better than him, too. We thought we were higher than them in all parts of our being—not just because of our skin color but because we were more benevolent, compassionate, and smarter. We thought we should be the ones to decide what mattered for both ourselves and them. We were the wise parents taking care of the poor, ignorant old infant-man who didn't know any better than to take a walk. We saw ourselves not only as a part of a nobler race but also as part of a better culture—we were from an elevated society. I didn't know it then, but we were really just lying to ourselves in a complicated way that involved us thinking about how great we were as opposed to how inferior they were. It was a two-for-one deal for us. I knew Daddy loved John as much as he ever loved anybody, but it seemed odd that he could love a colored man so much and still feel superior to him. Maybe what Daddy felt for John wasn't really love at all since it seems hard to truly love somebody when you feel better than them.

The townspeople also schooled me on how to feel about the coloreds. I remember hearing the word "nigger" being spoken out loud only once during my childhood. I don't think I heard the word too often because it was a shocking word to hear even in that time and place. I must have been around nine and was sleeping in town for the night, like so many other times. When I was staying in other people's homes, my life always depended on the rules of their houses, and sometimes I got into a few messes. I couldn't have been staying at Aunt Ernie's, Aunt Helen's, Aunt Della's, or Aunt Weggie's—they all would have kept me safe at home on a night like this one. I was probably sleeping over with one of my friends' families, but one thing is for sure, I didn't have any idea where my parents were or when I was going home. It was just another night like so many others when I was staying in town.

I can't remember hearing anybody call out "fire" or even walking down the street toward it, but I do recall standing in front of the house and watching it burn. It was a shocking thing to see because even though Daddy burned off fields after a harvest, I'd never seen a burning building. We had fires around Grand Tower occasionally, and we always drove by to look at the ashes when we came into town—but that was after the fact. Sometimes it was said they were started by barn burners. According to our way of thinking, barn burners are the worst kinds of people, since there's no cure for them. If somebody like that starts up in a small town he usually keeps going and causes all kinds of anxiety until he's found out. First you'd hear about a pile of trash catching fire in somebody's backyard, and then a shed or a barn would go up in flames. If they didn't catch him in time, before you knew it, he'd get somebody's house. But sooner or later the townspeople would figure out who it was, and they would unite behind a very strong movement to drive him out. I think it was just about the only thing they would never forgive—for us an arsonist was worse than a murderer because sometimes you could forgive a killer.

Watching the flames that night, it dawned on me that I was standing in the middle of a group of people that seemed like strangers. Grand Tower had a population of about eight hundred, and I knew most of their faces since I'd seen them my whole life. I did recognize a few people in the crowd, but it seemed like there were a lot of outsiders there that night. I squinted to see if maybe they looked different because the fire was casting an unnatural glow, and sure enough, a false glaring light from the flames was shining over the crowd, but most still looked like strangers. Some of them were yelping and shouting, and others stood silent. I heard a man say the n-word that I knew but couldn't remember ever hearing, but there was no way of telling where it came from. I caught myself staring at the people and had to look back toward the fire because everybody else was facing the blaze—it felt uncomfortable to be looking at the crowd instead of at the burning building.

It was a two-story wooden house on the edge of town that was always dilapidated and empty, but tonight it loomed larger and more meaningful than ever. There was a kind of awe about the spectacle that was starting to draw me in. It was spellbinding, and I felt like we were all becoming hypnotized by the power and magnitude of the fire glowing against the back sky. Then I recognized an older kid from my school standing next to me, so I asked her why people were cheering at a house on fire. She said that coloreds were going to move into the house, and they were coloreds with kids.

"The kids would be coming to school, so they had to burn it down."

I remember thinking, "Oh, I didn't know that. I didn't know it would be such a bad thing to have them in the school—so bad you'd have to burn a house down over it."

It was a hard thing to understand. I couldn't remember ever seeing any kids who were black, and for a second, I had to take in that there was such a thing. Black children didn't live in Grand Tower. But my eyes were drawn back to the crowd because they were starting to get more riled up. Some of them were ugly people, yelling out hateful words at the same time as they were laughing. Their pure meanness was awful. Eventually it seemed like a lot of folks were starting to feel uneasy, and they were moving away from the scene. I began to think about leaving myself—this was not like my family. We knew we were better than the coloreds, but some of these people just hated them with a vengeance—my family didn't hate them. In the end, it was a relief to get out of there. I walked away from the fire that night feeling confident that I was not only better than the coloreds, who wouldn't be moving into Grand Tower, but also above all these coarse, hateful white-trash people.

When I walked into the dining car that day on the train from Saint Louis to Kansas City, it wasn't a surprise to see another colored man waiting at the entrance. I knew they worked on the trains in the middle parts—the ones who waved to me from the front and the back ends were white, but in the center they were mostly colored.

Born by the River

I stood at the car door, struggling to hold my balance against the train with as much composure as a body could muster. The colored man was as straight as an arrow and didn't seem to be bothered by the trains jerking; he was dressed very neatly in white pants, a white jacket, and a black bow tie. After a while, I started to give up thinking he was going to seat me even though we were right next to each other; it was obvious that he must have seen me come in. Glancing over at him, I realized there was something about him and the porter that was very different from the old, colored people back home—neither one of them was taking much notice of me, and they had a similar manner that was starting to make me feel uncomfortable. I looked down at my purse and thought about going back to my seat since having a colored man in charge of me was not something I was used to, but it had been at least five hours since breakfast, and I was starving. Then my cousin in her bolero jacket and barrettes came to mind, so I stood up a little straighter and stuck my chin out the way she'd done when I offered to show her the chickens on Grandpa Wilson's farm. I looked directly at him thinking that he sure seemed to know what he was about, and then before you could say "boo," he had me seated at a four-top table with a white tablecloth and napkin that had been starched and ironed.

I sat down on the seat with sensations of relief and independence sweeping over me—my sixth-grade graduation was flashing through my mind again, and I was learning a thing or two about the world. The view out the window was pleasant with the farms and houses rushing by, and all of a sudden it seemed like there couldn't be anything better than that time and place—life was the best when you were sitting all alone in the dining car of a train with the world flying past you outside the window. But were we going too fast, I wondered—it looked like everything was flying by at an alarming speed. Being on a runaway train would scare the living daylights out of me—things could go south pretty fast in a situation like that.

But the waiter was watching, so it felt like I needed to stop worrying and decide what to do—he didn't seem like he was going to wait forever. Opening up the menu was another shocker; there were so many exotic and remarkable things listed on it: fruit cocktail, a thing called consommé, and tomato juice—it was just overwhelming. There were about a million choices all sorted out into different categories like appetizers, soups, and salads. I read everything very carefully while it dawned on me that the adults in my life must have always told me what to eat because I couldn't remember ever looking at a menu before—now that I was a grown-up, I'd have to start deciding things for myself. Then my eyes settled on the club sandwich, and I knew it was just the ticket since, after all, this was the club car—it seemed like the perfect thing to have. I put my order in with the waiter while I folded my napkin in a neat triangle on my lap and settled back to look out the window again. I was really hungry but didn't mind waiting for my food because of all that was going on around me.

My eyes must have gotten too comfortable gazing out the window, though, because as I look back now I can't remember how it all came to pass. They must have walked into the car and stood at the entrance waiting to be seated, but I didn't see them until it was too late. There was a quick little flurry of activity, and before I knew what happened, they were sitting directly across from me. It was a little girl who was a couple of years younger than me and her mother, and all of a sudden, they were right in front of me at my table. I remember noticing, through my shock, that both of them were dressed very nicely, and the mother had a neat little hat on. Their clothes unnerved me almost as much as their color. They sat very still and didn't move. Their stillness must have been contagious because right away I was frozen, too. I became terrified and couldn't budge an inch—it even felt like the train had stopped moving. Then my lunch arrived. Not one of us had said a word, nodded our heads, or even moved a finger. I tried to think about what I could or couldn't do while I looked down at my club sandwich. I wanted to eat it so badly but couldn't raise my hand to pick it up. After a few minutes all I could think about was that I needed to run away. Nobody had ever told me what to do in a situation like that.

Eight

It's not wise to violate the rules until
you know how to observe them.

—T. S. Eliot

If I could pick one person from my past to sit down and talk to today, it would be my aunt Liz. I would ask her, "Why did you always feel the need to control everybody in the family? Did you really hate Mother as much as it seemed? Have you ever felt sorry for what you did to us?"

As soon as the train started slowing down for the station in Kansas City, I remembered that she would want to give me a big hug and kiss, which was something I despised doing; nobody on either side of the family ever felt the need to greet one another that way. Kissing and hugging her was even more aggravating when you considered that it always took some time to get used to being around her, and the hugging and kissing part came at that first second when you were with her. You just never had a chance to collect yourself.

Born by the River

Suddenly the train jerked to a stop, and there she was standing on the platform with her crazy bird dog, Missy. The dog was jumping and pulling on its leash, and I thought about how Daddy was right—a dog like that should not be kept locked up in a house in town, never mind on a leash. Who on earth even had a dog leash? I couldn't remember ever seeing one on any other dog but hers. Daddy kept over ten hound dogs on the island, plus we had a Dalmatian in the house, and we didn't own one leash.

After she grabbed me and forced me to hug and kiss her, we got into the car, and the world slowed down to her maddening pace. There wouldn't be one enjoyable minute for a whole week—the food we ate, the way we ate it, the place where I'd have to sleep, her friends, the insane asylum where she worked, and her dog—everything would be completely miserable for me. I was trapped, and there would be no way out. Daddy's words, "Be nice to your aunt Liz and respect your elders," rang in my ears while I sat in the car trying to answer her nosy questions. Mostly I didn't know anything about the stuff she wanted to hear—things about Mother and Daddy and the island. She and her sister, my other old-maid aunt who lived out in California, owned the same amount of the island as Daddy, but I couldn't see how that made our lives any of their business—plus I didn't care about any of the things she wanted to know.

If she knew enough to ask I could have told her about going down to the old barn at the far end of the horse pasture—I'd even jumped out of the hayloft a few times, and that was really fun. Or I could talk about riding my bicycle into the backwoods and finding a peaceful spot that had been cleared in the trees. And then there was the tornado that had whipped through the yard this spring. I went outside and ran around the house three times before somebody called me in—the wind was blowing harder than the dickens, and it was terrifying. Or what about the time Daddy took me fishing on the other side of the levee? I'll never forget the thrill of finding a beautiful spot along the river that I didn't even know existed, right there on the island. Most likely it was already gone, since the river had probably washed it away. We could've talked about deer season, which was coming up, and how everybody would want to kill Zorro, the giant deer that was a legend on the island. But if I mentioned that, she'd ask me how it would make me feel to have Zorro killed, and then I'd be uncomfortable again. It was better not to tell her anything.

After we left the train station, the first thing we did was drive to a field where she let her dog out to run. We stood on the side of the road for half an hour and watched her stupid dog run like a crazy thing up and down the pasture. It didn't seem to calm her down any, though; she was crazier than ever when we got back into the car. Then we drove to the parking lot of a drugstore. Aunt Liz turned the car off and looked at me for a minute or two, not saying a word.

It was just like her to do something like that. She always talked very slowly and would pause for a few seconds in the middle of her sentences. It was amazing what a powerful effect a little thing like that could have on somebody—it just drove you crazy. I'd seen her do it all the time to my parents, and it had the effect of making them look angry while she seemed calm and in control of the situation—maybe that was one of the reasons she won every argument. The images of those contentious times are burned in my mind—of lying in bed every Christmas Eve while I worried that Santa wouldn't come if they didn't stop arguing about money. Mother and Aunt Liz both smoked, so there was twice as much cigarette smoke hanging in the house as normal—it was the only thing they had in common. Everything else about them was different. Mother would be wearing high heels and an attractive cocktail dress with a big necklace, and Aunt Liz would be in sturdy shoes and a boxy tweed suit with a three-stranded pearl necklace around her neck. Mother's right hand would be waving in the air above her head while she talked, then she would rest her fingers on the top of her hair into a kind of crown while her elbow was extended out—Aunt Liz would not be moving an inch. All this would be going on while Daddy was getting more and more aggravated by the minute.

"Do you need anything from the drugstore?" she finally asked, snapping my mind back into the car with her. I felt frozen and kept my eyes locked on the dashboard straight ahead of me.

"No, thank you."

I thought I knew what she was asking me about but wasn't 100 percent sure. At that time, I didn't have a name for it or know there was something for it in the drugstore. I just used toilet paper to get by the best way I could. It was messy, but it worked, and after a few days the whole thing was past.

"Your mother should be talking to you about these things."

There was a long pause.

"You ought to ask her," she said as she drove off.

It was just like her to know all your secrets.

Finally, we got to her house, and it was a relief not to be trapped in the car with her any more. It was a close call, though, because just as she turned into her driveway she looked at me and said, "You know, I have never even gotten enough money from the island to buy a car." But by then we had stopped, so I was able to open the door and jump out. Later on, when I went to the bathroom I realized that my dress was soiled. I'd have to look around for some Kleenex—the toilet paper wasn't working too well. Then I changed my underpants and hid the dirty ones in the back of a drawer.

Her house was a small bungalow on Randolph Street in Topeka, Kansas. It had a long room that she used as a living room on one end and a dining room on the other. In the back were two small bedrooms—one with a bed and the other with a TV. Off the dining room was a little kitchen. The basement was paneled in wood and had a small bedroom where I always slept. In the paneled room, there was a fake little fireplace surrounded by a bunch of books. The basement was always a refuge for me, and when she figured out I was reading her books, she started leaving me alone down there. One book I picked up that really amazed me was *The Feminine Mystique.* It made me think about the women in my own family—my mother, Aunt Liz, and my grandmother. Only Grandma seemed like she was stuck the same way the women in the book were. It was interesting, but I didn't get past the first few chapters—there wasn't much free time since I spent the week doing all the usual things that Aunt Liz thought were so important.

A friend of hers came by to keep me company during the day while she worked. That was better than spending my time cooped up in her secretary's office at the mental hospital like I used to do. Her friend and I went to a few dusty museums and some parks. One day we had lunch at a place where you could stay in your car and have the food delivered to you; it was the first time I ever remember eating a hamburger—we mostly ate ham or pimento cheese sandwiches at home.

In the afternoons, Aunt Liz came home and started in on me with some important things she thought I needed to know about. During this visit she was set on linens. She dug out all her monogrammed tablecloths and taught me how to wash and fold them. The big thing was that when I ironed them, I had to make sure I only ironed them on the back of the monogram while it was facedown in a clean white washcloth. That way, the monogram would "pop out," according to her. Then she got out a bunch of old photo albums and started matching up the monograms with the people's pictures. They were mostly photos of Roths with a few Clarks turning up once in a while. I didn't know much about the Clarks, and that shocked her to no end. She paused for a really long time while she stared at me. It felt like I had turned into something she was trying to figure out how to clean up.

"Your Grandfather Clark, my father...was born in New Hampshire in 1847. He was a descendant, one hundred percent, of New England Puritans. He is a direct descendant of over thirty original New Hampshire and Massachusetts families."

I had heard a little bit of this stuff already but wanted her to stop staring at me, so I kept my eyes down and didn't say anything. Finally, she left the room, but pretty soon she came back with a folder of papers for me to read—then she said she'd ask me about them later. I went down to the basement as soon as possible and started looking through the file. Her writing was always hard to read, but a lot of the papers were typed out, so that made it easier. I was happy to go through them because it was better to read by myself than to listen to her lecturing.

Thankfully it wasn't too boring because there was a lot of pretty interesting stuff in there. It was kind of like the Bible because it was surprising that grown-ups would let kids read about such things. I quickly found the first man on the Clark side to come to America. His name was Stephen Bachiler, and he came over from England in 1632 when he was seventy-two years old. He'd gone to Oxford University and was a preacher and brought some of his congregation with him. He got into trouble right away with the Puritans by refusing to swear allegiance to the Crown of England. In the dead of winter, he had to walk a hundred miles from Ipswich, Massachusetts, to Barnstable on Cape Cod. Then his wife died, and his house burned. He sued some people in the town who wouldn't pay him for being a preacher. Then everybody thought it was weird that he was living alone with another woman named Mary who was his young housekeeper, so the townspeople made him marry her when he was eighty-seven years old. Two years later, she tried to divorce him, but the court refused. After that, she started going out with a sailor named George Rogers. Mary and George ran off to Maine, where they got caught. They were beaten, and she was branded with the capital letter A. Finally, Stephen went back to England when he was ninety-four years old. He died six years later when he was one hundred years old. Then a man named Nathaniel Hawthorne wrote a book about it.

The other thing I found was about a witch trial for a woman named Goody Cole. A bunch of our relatives testified against her at the trial in 1656. She was sent to a prison in Boston, and then the next year there was a big shipwreck where a lot of people from the town died. Everyone thought the wreck happened because she cursed them.

The one I liked best, though, was a man named Robert Pike who wrote an essay about how silly the Salem witch trials were. He started the ball rolling that stopped all those hysterical girls from accusing people of being with Satan. I wondered what he would say to the prissy girls at school who always wore barrettes.

After a while, the reading became tiresome, so I went upstairs to see what kind of torture would be waiting for me next. I was surprised to see Aunt Liz watching TV, which was a big relief since TV was one of the things you missed the most at her house—she never turned it on. I was disappointed soon enough, though, to realize she was only watching the news about a colored man who was making a speech to a big group of people. This seemed strange to me—why would anybody put a colored man on television? I'd never seen one talking in an important way like that before; in a way that made you think people were listening to him. I caught a few of his words, but they didn't make much sense. It was easier to turn away in disgust than it was to try to figure it out. But right away I could feel she had a problem with me having any kind of way of thinking that wasn't set by her.

Pretty soon she said, "Why don't you listen to what he is saying and see what you think about it?"

I wasn't used to having a grown-up ask me what I thought about something, but maybe that's what happened after you graduated from the sixth grade. I looked back at the TV and started to listen to him. It didn't seem like he was talking about anything outrageous or something you could disagree with, but at the same time I felt like she was laying a trap for me.

He said, "Now is the time to make justice a reality for all of God's children."

"What do you think about that?" she asked me.

Her questions always made me feel cornered because I knew she was trying to get me to change something about myself or to learn some new thing. I didn't answer her right away since talking to her seemed like more work than trying to understand what he was saying. So I just kept listening to him.

"Does it sound reasonable to you?"

It was hard to understand all his words, but something about it sounded like the truth because I was starting to see for myself that a lot of the rules about colored people didn't add up—and it was good that he was talking about the children. But then he seemed like he was unhappy about things. Nobody ever told me that people were upset about how it was between the whites and the coloreds, so the idea that there needed to be a change had never come to me. Even though I watched that house burn, none of this ever crossed my mind. I didn't know what to believe except that the grown-ups had created the world, not me—I was just trying to get by, and it didn't seem like that was getting any easier.

"Yeah, I guess it makes sense," I finally said, without looking at her. I didn't want to talk to my aunt Liz about any of this business or anything else, but if I was supposed to respect old, colored people the same as old, white people, then why couldn't the kids come to school? If the old folks could live in town, why couldn't the kids live there? How old did the blacks have to be to live in town with the whites? It was just one more example of things not being fair for the kids. My thoughts went back to the mother and daughter on the train—could

I have eaten my sandwich with just the mother there? I didn't know how it was all supposed to work.

After a week I said good-bye to Aunt Liz. I think that summer was the last time I stayed at her house and the last chance she had to school me on life. I never got the chance to talk to her as an adult or to tell her how much she shaped who I turned out to be. Aunt Liz never knew what she ended up meaning to me. When she asked me what I thought about things, it taught me I could think for myself and form my own opinions and that it was all right to question what I'd been told. Now I can see she was truly my only lifeline to the world outside my little hometown. In the end, I kept all her linens and antiques, and I'll always think about her when I'm ironing a napkin. Sometimes, when I'm in a museum, I remember the dusty cases of artifacts we used to look over in Topeka and how she always asked me what I noticed about them. But it wasn't educating me about linens or taking me to museums that made the big difference in my life, and her influence on me wasn't as a role model or a mentor, even though she was a very liberated and educated woman at the top of her field. I see now that her biggest value to me was how she pushed me out of my narrow upbringing and into the changing world that was unfolding in the second half of the twentieth century. When I think about how different my life would have been without her own particular style of love and upbringing, I'm grateful.

Elizabeth Jenness Clark, circa 1957

Nine

Where is the life we lost living?

—T. S. ELIOT

A fter my week with Aunt Liz, she drove me to Kansas City to pass me off to Daddy. I thanked her and ran over to his truck as fast as my legs could go. He'd parked under a shade tree, so it wasn't too hot inside the truck; then the two of them stood under another tree and talked. They were trying to keep their voices down, but a few words were louder than others—words like "irresponsibly," "island," and "this can't continue." I heard her ask him if she had his word on something and knew that wasn't right. Whatever he said was as good as gold—it was an insult to ask him to give his word. She should have known that, but she didn't; it was like she didn't know anything.

When Daddy finally got in and started driving he seemed upset, but I didn't have too much sympathy for him because I'd just spent a whole week with Aunt Liz. You always felt kind of beaten up after *you were around her; I just wanted him to drive faster so we could get away as quickly as possible.*

On our way home from Kansas City that day, we drove through the town where Daddy had grown up: Mexico, Missouri.

"You remember the barn, don't you?" he said when we passed by the old building in Mexico that was like a church to our family. We always drove past it and took a long look.

The run-down stable had a buckle in the wood along one side, and you would think it was going to fall over any minute. It was hard to imagine that such a sorry old building was so important to the family, but I knew enough not to point that out. The words, "Simmons' Stables" were painted on the front, since they were the owners now. It made Daddy feel good to talk about all this old stuff, so I pretended like I hadn't heard it before. He told me again about how it was built during the golden age of the American Saddlebred Horse—they were the high-stepping horses with the arched necks that were a must for rich and powerful people before the car was invented. He said that the horses were used for riding and in a harness to pull a buggy. American Saddle Horses are known as the "peacocks of the horse world," and Mexico, Missouri, was once the American Saddle Horse capital of the world.

"They are beautiful horses that have several gaits and speeds," he said. "The Simmons' stable over there was built by your grandpa. Did you know that? He gave Tom Bass his first job."

I knew about Tom Bass, the black horseman who was born a slave. He was one of the first black men to compete in a sport with whites—the one who'd made history when he invented the Bass Bit. It's a good bit because it's a lot easier on the horses' mouths—Daddy had shown them to me when we tended to the horses on the island.

"They sold the best horses in the country—to presidents, queens, and even 'Buffalo Bill' Cody. People from all over the world came to his barn to buy horses."

Belle Beach, Tom Bass up; Cyrus F. Clark, owner

After the visit to the barn Daddy didn't say anything about where we were going next, and I didn't need to ask. The truck felt like an old dog finding its way home as it seemed to drive itself through the town, turning this way or that. Pretty soon we were passing under the big arched sign "ELMWOOD CEMETERY" and then down the bumpy dirt road that led to the Clark plot. Even though he'd been dead for over twenty-eight years, my grandfather, Cyrus F. Clark, still held the family's reigns tightly, and you could always feel them draw up on you when you neared his grave—the closer you came to his marker, the tighter the pull.

Cyrus F. Clark Sr.

After a minute of stillness it felt like we'd offered up the right amount of respect. I was at ease enough to glance around at the other Clark graves in the plot. Growing up, a cemetery was always an interesting place to be for me because of all the relatives who were buried there. They were important to the family—it seemed like it didn't matter whether you were dead or alive; if you were part of the family you still counted for something. The cemetery on Walker Hill in Grand Tower had all the Wilsons and Poes, while this one had the Clarks.

Most of the headstones were worn, and you could barely make out what they said. But I could read enough of them to be entertained while Daddy pulled weeds around the burial plots. My favorite markers were the two that mentioned the Civil War. I always looked at those first. They were my grandfather's brothers, and they'd fought in Ohio regiments for the Union. I stood over Jacob Pike Clark's grave and imagined him in there with only one arm—the other had been blown off in West Virginia. The marker said he was born in 1841 and died in 1877, so he survived the war but still died when he was only thirty-six years old. He was the one who had gone west to become the land register for the Washington Territory.

The other marker that had an Ohio regiment listed on it was for John Everett Clark. Daddy said they both joined up with the Union army while the family lived in Ohio where they owned a farm—they lived there for a few years on their way from New Hampshire to Missouri. John Everett survived the war just like Jacob Pike, but he died fairly young out in San Francisco at the age of forty-four.

"So they brought his body all the way back here?" I asked Daddy. "How did they do that?"

"On a train," he said. "You're curious about your relatives all of a sudden."

I told him Aunt Liz had me reading up on the family when I was in Topeka and that some of them seemed kind of interesting. Then I started asking him questions. He told me all kinds of things that sounded like what Aunt Liz said, but it was a lot more interesting to hear this from him. Back in the truck, we talked about them while we drove through Saint Louis and until I fell asleep.

The family had come out west in 1855 after living for over two hundred years in New Hampshire and Massachusetts. When they first came to America, they were Puritans—they founded a town called Hampton, New Hampshire. Almost all of them were farmers. One of them, Frances Jenness, had a state park named after him in New Hampshire. In the two hundred years they'd spent in New England, there had been over thirty families in New Hampshire and Massachusetts and ten generations from 1632 to 1855.

Daddy talked about a lot of things I didn't understand. But the word "Puritan" seemed to come up a lot, and I remembered Aunt Liz made a big deal about it. I didn't dare ask her what it meant because if I ever showed an interest in anything she wanted me to know, a floodgate would open, and pretty soon I would be drowning before I knew what hit me. But with Daddy it was safe, so I asked him what the word meant. When he started to explain what a Puritan was, we got to talking about how they weren't anything like the people in Grand Tower, Saint Louis, or Mexico. They were different, Daddy said, but being different paid off for his dad. Being a New Englander, living in Ohio, and getting a good education gave him a leg up in Missouri. He ended up owning one of the banks in town, starting the horse business, and then he was elected to the Missouri legislature. But all this talk got me wondering why they came west after two hundred years of living in the east.

It didn't seem like a good idea when you looked back on what a mess it turned out to be for them. Of course they didn't know that the Civil War was going to start up only six years after they left—if they'd known that they probably wouldn't have stopped in a dangerous place like Amelia, Ohio, for the war years. Amelia was right across the border from Kentucky and got raided all the time by Confederate soldiers like General Morgan and his cavalrymen. Luckily, my grandfather was born in 1847 and was only fourteen when the war started. He went to school during those years and became a teacher instead of fighting. After the war he went to Texas and taught at the King Ranch for a while; on his way back east he traveled up to the Washington Territory to visit his brother. Then he got a job teaching in Mexico, Missouri, and the rest of the family moved from Ohio to join him.

The Clarks were lucky for a while, but even without any of them dying in the Civil War, it seemed like death followed them wherever they went. Their oldest daughter, Betsy, died in Ohio when she was only twenty-five. Then in 1867, a few years after the war ended, they moved to Missouri. In 1869 another daughter died when she was twenty-five too—just like her sister Betsy. In 1872 it was the Dad's time—he was sixty-one. Jacob Pike, the one who lost his arm in West Virginia, was gone by age thirty-six.

There was a lot of dying, and it made me feel a little depressed. I thought back to all the dead Roths who used to live in Saint Louis—but at least they made it to old age. All my dad's aunts and uncles on the Clark side died so young. But Daddy wasn't finished—his most interesting uncle was Oliver Decatur, who died at forty-eight in Deadwood, South Dakota, of typhoid fever. I perked up when he mentioned Deadwood—I'd heard about that town from cowboy movies. Daddy laughed when I said, "That was where Calamity Jane and Wild Bill Hickok lived. Wild Bill got shot there! Did Oliver know Wild Bill?" But Daddy didn't know if Oliver knew Wild Bill, he said that maybe he could have.

We talked on about Wild Bill for a while and then went back to the Clarks. There was more tragedy to be told because in 1887 another son, John Everett, died in San Francisco at forty-four. So we figured out that John Clark and his wife, who was the first Elizabeth Jenness Clark (with me being the third after Aunt Liz), came west from New Hampshire in 1855 with their seven children, and five out of the seven died under the age of fifty. None of those five ever had any children.

I decided that they should have never come out west—what a heap of trouble it was for them. But Daddy pointed out that neither one of us would be here if they hadn't because his dad would never have met his mom in Saint Louis. That made a lot of sense to me.

"Your daddy didn't die so young did he?" I asked him.

I remembered the answer to that question as soon as it popped out of my mouth because now we were talking about Daddy's parents, and I knew a lot about them. Cyrus F. Clark couldn't have died young since he'd had two complete families—he and his first wife had two children before she died, and then he married Sophie Margaretha Roth in 1906 when she was thirty-seven and he was fifty-eight.

An older husband didn't mean he was a father figure to her, though, because she kept her independence by buying several farms around Mexico—they were always called Miss Sophie's places. And she stuck with her own politics too—for years she headed up the Women's Republican League while her husband was a Democrat who had once served in the Missouri House of Representatives.

By the time my grandparents married, Sophie's father—Adam Roth—had been dead for six years and her mother for four. She and her seven unmarried brothers and sisters lived on in the Locust Street house in Saint Louis for another four years before selling it. In 1906—the same year that Sophie and Cyrus married—her youngest sister, Beulah, married George Barker from Banning, California. Two years later, Sophie had twins: one was my Aunt Margaretha who lived out in California while I was growing up, and the other one was a boy who died. Then came Aunt Liz in 1910 and Daddy in 1911.

We didn't talk for some time after that, so I looked over at Daddy to see what was going on. I could tell he was upset, and it felt like he was going to start saying I should marry a Clark so we could carry on the family name. But he only did that when he was drunk. The trouble was all this business with Aunt Liz, the island, and money— those things had always been thorns, but this time was different. This time I felt like something was going to happen. All of a sudden I was crying. I turned my head to look out the window thinking about how I didn't even have the chance to hold back my tears—they'd just started. It seemed like I couldn't control anything, even my own self, much less all this business with the grown-ups who went on and on with all their problems; they messed up everything they could get their hands on. I wanted to ask Daddy if Aunt Liz was going to make us sell the island, but I couldn't. I didn't want to know the answer, and he would see that I was crying if I tried to talk. It was an impossible thing to think about because selling the island would be the end of everything—our home, our family, and Daddy. When I glanced over his way, I could see that the life was already starting to drain out of him.

The island was everything to Daddy, and I knew they would have to destroy him before he would give it up. His own two sisters would have to strip off every part of his being—his freedom, pride, home, family, and spirit—to get what they wanted. Sure, maybe this was all happening because of his drinking, but for me that was just a small part of who he was. Nobody was looking at what was important, and all of them—Mother, Daddy, Aunt Liz, and Aunt Margaretha—they all seemed to be part of the mess that was heading our way. It was as if they had us loaded into a boat without any oars, and we were being swept downriver in a swift current.

Ten

I said to my soul, be still, and wait without hope,
for hope would be hope for the wrong thing.

—T. S. ELIOT

I woke up when Daddy's truck turned off the highway and onto the road that led into town. Pretty soon we would be crossing over the railroad tracks, and then, finally, we'd be back in Grand Tower. I could feel the town stretching off to our right and the river flowing next to it. My imagination flew out the truck window and then up and down the streets past all the houses that were so familiar me; I thought about all the aunts, uncles, cousins, friends, the man who owned the bank, and the family that ran the grocery store. They were all there asleep in their beds. I flew down by Aunt Helen's and then to the Presbyterian Church, over Uncle Stacy and Aunt Ernie's house, and turned left by the old schoolhouse. Then I came back up Front Street by Keller's store, the bank, the old movie theater, and passed by Daddy's favorite tavern. I got back into the truck just in time to be there when he turned left onto the levee road. We climbed up the slope

to the top of the levee while the gravel popped up underneath the floor
boards of the truck. I sat up and opened my eyes just in time to see the
moon shining on the chute—it was a clear night, and the water that
surrounded the island sparkled. The chute curved to the right, and
the reflection of the trees that grew along the shore formed a dark and
jagged line. Then I flew out of the truck again and followed the chute
around in a circle. I traveled along the three miles of water that sur-
rounded the island until it hit the levee road again. Then my mind
came back down the levee to where we were driving. I was back in the
truck with Daddy in time to see the two tall cottonwood trees that grew
halfway between our house and the chute. At that point, our house
was visible in the distance. We were home again, at last. There was
a light shining in the house, so the generator was still on, but other
than that, it was all emptiness as far as you could see.

No one lived on the island but us. Nobody had any business coming to it unless they wanted to see one of our family.
Sometimes a car would drive down the levee, but we just figured it was a looky-loo who wanted to go to Missouri without
crossing the Mississippi—there weren't too many ways you
could get from Illinois to Missouri without crossing the river.
Other than that, it was just us except during the day when
the field hands came out to work. Every once in a while they
stayed overnight when they needed to sleep it off in a shed,
but that didn't happen too often.

It was about this time that I saw the movie *State Fair* in
Cape Girardeau. In the opening scene everybody was singing

and having fun on a farm; they all seemed so happy—jumping out of haylofts and riding around on horses. Even the cows and chickens were over the moon. All that hustle and bustle seemed like the most wonderful thing you could ever imagine. As the movie went along, the fun had me mesmerized until I was green with envy. And then it hit me: I already lived on a farm. We had barns with haylofts, ponds, and even horses—it would be so easy to make it perfect by adding just a few animals like chickens and pigs. They were easy to take care of—Grandma did it all by herself on Grandpa Wilson's farm. I could see my older sister jumping out of a hayloft into the arms of some cute boyfriend—she would love having a real farm. I imagined just how it would be—we would be eating our breakfast some morning and look out the window to see that my pet pig had escaped from his pen. Then I would run outside and shoo him back through the gate, and our dogs would be running around barking. Pretty soon, the dogs would help me out, and everybody would laugh. In the summer, we would race around the fields on horses and then ride down to the chute to jump in for a swim. After that, we could ride through the woods and look for deer and bobcats—with three thousand acres surrounded by water, we could do almost anything we wanted. It would be even better than the movie because we had an endless amount of space all to ourselves—having an island was better than anything. It was a wonderful plan and wouldn't take much to make real. I was sure Daddy would love the idea, and Mother wouldn't have to do anything, so she wouldn't care about having a few chickens. Anyway, there were plenty of hired hands around to help out, and I loved doing stuff with them, so it would all be perfect. I was thinking about this a lot during those times—it was a dream that had me caught up in its net.

I always thought about Mom, our old housekeeper, when I walked through the front door of our home. I thought about her at that moment because of the time when I came in from school one day and couldn't find her. I asked Mother where she was. "Mom moved out—you don't need her anymore. You're too old," she said.

And that was it. That was the end of Mom—the woman who had worked for our family ever since I was a baby. She cooked and cleaned for us, and when I was seven years old she nursed me through the whooping cough for two months. She lived on the island off and on for around ten years, and that brought a lot of stability to our lives. It was great to have her around, but she wasn't always there since, like most women, she wouldn't spend the night alone on the island because it was too isolated. So when my parents were gone, as they often were, I still had to stay in town with friends or relatives. I longed for Mom during those times as much as I missed being at home.

She was a frail woman who had her own way of doing things, and it was said that she was part Cherokee Indian.

Born by the River

There were a lot of Cherokees around the area because the northern route of the Trail of Tears passed only a few miles south of Grand Tower.

During the winter of 1838 to 1839 five thousand Indians were being forced to walk from their homes in North Carolina to an Indian reservation in Oklahoma. On the way to Oklahoma they got stuck in Ware, Illinois, for months because ice on the river made it impossible for them to cross to the Missouri side. Hundreds of them never made it to Oklahoma—they either died or ended up staying in the area. At school, a lot of kids on the playground used to brag about having Cherokee Indian blood in their veins, and the rest of us were always impressed. Indian blood was something to be very proud of in Southern Illinois. Mom seemed to carry some of those hard times around with her.

We called her *Mom*, but her real name was Myrtle Black. Mom had an uncanny sense of most things, but she wasn't quick to share her thoughts with people. She went about her business in a tight-lipped way that called up respect from others, and she had a quiet tolerance for her situation in life that sometimes came off as reserved aloofness. Playing solitaire was her favorite pastime when she found a minute of rest between taking care of me, cooking for the hired hands, and cleaning up. Quiet passed over the house when she sat at the table in the dining room, turning her cards faceup and carefully studying the board. There was something about growing up in a house with a wise old woman sitting and playing solitaire while the clock ticked.

At that time there was no telephone or television on the island, and during the day the generator would be off, so time would pass with a stillness that went unnoticed. Sometimes, if the weather was good, we would go out on a "ramble," as she called them. On a ramble, the two of us would wander around the fields and roads that were closest to the house and forage for special things she wanted to find. In the spring, a big treat for her was pokeweed because she liked to put it in salads. During the fall, we would go into the woods and look for old tree stumps where you could find morel mushrooms hidden in the wet leaves next to decaying wood. Morel mushrooms were the greatest treat in the world according to Mom. But, then again, pretty much everything had an important meaning to her. Mostly her mind was set on things that were peculiar, and they whirled around in her brain and then got connected to one superstition or another. Superstitions were like a religion for her. To Mom, a light in the distance was a phantom light that meant somebody was going to die, which seemed logical on the island because there weren't any neighbors' lights to see. A mysterious glow on the horizon was an unnatural thing that made your imagination fly, and with Mom around to stoke your fears, it was easy to conjure up all kinds of scary things. She taught me all the superstitious rules about life, like how you could never put a hat on the bed or an umbrella up in the house because bad luck would quickly follow. The list seemed infinite and covered just about everything there ever was—salt, cats, ladders, birds, sweeping, mirrors, hands itching, and on and on. According to Mom, these were things you had to know in order to avoid the troubles of the world.

But I know now that she was wrong—if only life was that simple and there really was a way to stave off all your troubles. How perfect everything would be if superstitions worked or if a Pat Boone fantasy movie could come true. But my real life was much more complicated than a dream about a movie or an old woman playing solitaire while the clock ticked. For me, there was never going to be a barnyard full of pets or a family laughing. No matter how careful I was to hold on to her superstitions or make wishes in my head, a happy family was not to be.

Eleven

We all do no end of feeling, and
we mistake it for thinking.

—Mark Twain

My parents moved permanently onto the island in 1949.
At the time of my birth in 1951 the levee from the mainland was unfinished, so a few months before my due date they moved back into town in case Mother had another troubled delivery. At that time the island was still an island. Without any neighbors, telephone, or electricity it was too dangerous for them to stay there during the last few months of her pregnancy because getting into Grand Tower took hours. First you had to hitch the wagon to the tractor and then ride over a mile down the muddy dirt road to the river. Once on the bank, you gathered up all your gear and hoped the quicksand didn't get you before you piled into a skiff. After that you had to cross the narrow body of water we called "the chute" to the Illinois side, and if you were rowing, you needed to watch out

for water moccasins slithering up the oars and into the boat. Then it was another mile into town in the pickup truck that was always left waiting along the shoreline.

People's attitudes about giving birth out on farms had changed since the time when my grandmother delivered her oldest daughter, Nettie, on the island over thirty years earlier. Besides the remoteness of the place, a bigger concern was that when I was due, my parents were the only family living there—all the Poes and Wilsons had long since moved into Grand Tower or Wittenberg.

After a few months of living in town, her delivery time came, and Doc Hughes was called in. She had a long night of it at my grandmother's house—the same place where she had been born twenty-seven years earlier, but the birth was tough in more ways than one.

Mother said she first realized Daddy had a serious drinking problem on the night I was born, but it's hard to imagine she didn't know it sooner since by that time they had been married for five years. Maybe the sad truth came to her when she saw him drunk while she was struggling to have their baby or maybe the real story was that he had the biggest binge of his life when he laid eyes on me.

Daddy told me later, "When I realized you were a girl I wanted to throw either myself or you into the river."

I never held it against him, though, because I grew to understand why he felt that way. I knew before I was too old how strongly his hopes for holding on to the island were tied to me being a boy and why it was all on me because after those earlier miscarriages Doc Hughes said there wasn't much chance she would ever have another baby. To help the situation, when she was pregnant with me, Doc recommended that she start smoking to see if it would still her nerves enough to keep the baby.

In the meantime, Daddy waited anxiously to see if they would have a boy or a girl. Having a boy meant everything to him because he was like so many men from those times—he thought owning land and passing it down through the male line was the most important thing in the world. He was part of an age-old tradition that held fiercely to the idea that you had to own property in order to secure a future for your family. Nothing else was really worth anything according to this custom. He would point out that the Roths had bought farms outside of Saint Louis as investments even though they made their fortune through trade, and every prominent family in Mexico had a family farm somewhere out in the county that had been farmed for generations. He was always trying to drum the importance of owning land into us any way he could. And more than once he brought up the kings and queens of England as examples. Daddy said if anybody ever asked the British royal family about their occupation, they always answered that they were farmers.

"There is no higher calling than owning land. It's more important than being a king," he would say.

My father thought it was a shame so many of the Clark farms had been sold after his dad died—he said that Cyrus F. Clark Sr. would never have approved. He was fiercely trying to keep this one last piece of land and knew that without a son to inherit the island it would be hard to keep Aunt Liz and Aunt Margaretha from selling. A pall was cast over the family when I was born because a girl meant the future would be very uncertain. With my birth, everybody saw the writing on the wall—my dad had just lost his chance of ever persuading his sisters to keep the island because there was a boy in the family who might want to farm it someday. Aunt Liz lived in Topeka, Kansas, and Aunt Margaretha was way out in California, so they weren't interested in tying up their money in land that had so little yield. Aunt Liz and Aunt Margaretha didn't share Daddy's strong, almost religious feelings about the value of holding on to such a rare piece of property. In fact, they seemed to begrudge us for wanting to keep it. Plus, they downright resented Daddy's drinking and Mother's flamboyant ways. But the island was the most valuable thing in the world to my dad, and since I was raised to think the same way, I never questioned his feelings.

My parents first met on a farm in Audrain County, Missouri, when Mother was about twelve and Daddy was in his midtwenties. It was toward the end of the Depression, but the Poe family was doing pretty well because my mother's father, Wamp Poe, was a third-generation riverboat captain on the Mississippi. They were living in Cape Girardeau, Missouri, at the time and had come up to Mexico to visit relatives on the Wilson side. But things were about to fall apart for the Poes because her father was in the thick of falling in love with another woman, and the two of them were laying plans for him to leave his wife and children. By that time, my mother's parents had lost four of their eight children—two in the same week—so it's not hard to imagine they had a troubled marriage. Those tragedies plus the long stretches of time rivermen spent away from home had taken a toll on their lives.

After her husband left her, my grandmother returned to Grand Tower where she took odd jobs as a nurse around town while she struggled to hold things together. Her oldest daughter, Nettie, would be fine since by that time she was married to Maximillian Joseph Koeck, the son of a well-to-do German brewing family in Cape Girardeau. Her son, Rainey, was all right—he could go on living with her parents on the Wilson farm across the river in Missouri; he'd lived with them off and on since grade school. But her other two children, Marion and Edgar Allen, were still living at home and had to be looked after. At that time, divorce was almost unheard of in those parts, so it was a huge stigma for my grandmother and her two children. But she managed things well enough over the next few years with the help of her large extended family of Poes and Wilsons who lived on both sides of the river. She made it work as well as she could until the world's problems started to flood into Grand Tower.

When Pearl Harbor was bombed in December of 1941 my mother, Marion Francis Poe, was seventeen years old and a senior in high school. To her it seemed like the world had turned upside down, and suddenly everybody was doing something thrilling or going someplace interesting. She was young and pretty with dark-brown hair and beautiful gray-blue eyes. She was ready to be swept away by the excitement of the war; she longed to be part of the events that were quickly connecting Grand Tower to the rest of the world. Like every other place in the country, the insulated little river town was suddenly swirling with world problems that were about to change things forever. My mother's life had already been crushed by her parents' divorce, so without the stable footing of family, she did the only thing that seemed in her power to do—she quit high school and married a boy named Bill Paul who was set to go to war in a few weeks. They barely knew each other, but it seemed like the right time to do something dramatic, and there weren't too many choices available to her. After a quick marriage, he left for the war. She quit high school to go to work in Saint Louis making bomber sights— she would live with her Poe relatives and work there for two years. But even in the big city, she still felt like she was missing something. Next she tried living in Dallas for a few months with other relatives, but things weren't working out too well for her there, either. In December of 1944 she was coming home on a train for Christmas when she saw a glamorous soldier from the Women's Army Corps. Mother was struck by the WAC's self-confidence and impressive uniform, and by the time they arrived in Saint Louis she'd decided to join the army herself. A few months later she was sent to Fort Des Moines in Iowa for six weeks of basic training, and after that she was stationed in Wichita Falls, Texas, where she worked in an office and helped outfit soldiers with clothes and gear for their next assignments. By that time, it was 1945 and the war was almost over.

Marion Poe Paul, 1945

After Germany surrendered in September of that year, her husband, Bill Paul, was discharged from the army. When he came back to Illinois she got a pass to join him in Grand Tower, and during the furlough she became pregnant with my sister—that was the last time they would be together. After her leave she returned to the army in Texas, and Bill moved into his parents' home. Then, right before Christmas, the army discharged her for being pregnant, and she was back in Grand Tower living with her mother—by that time Bill was done with the marriage and wanted a divorce. In later years she was always reluctant to talk about Bill Paul and never pined for him—there weren't any sad looks or long signs about a lost love, and she never had any resentment or anger. She would always say—without emotion or sorrow—that they were too young to get married in the first place, and they barely knew each other. Then she would add that divorce wasn't such a big deal in those days because the old stigmas about it were changing with all the quick wartime marriages falling apart. It was easy to understand why she never wanted those times dredged up, since she had moved on, but it also mirrored her devil-may-care attitude about life in general—the past was always in the past for her; you never cried over spilled milk. And besides, who cared about a divorce when there was the thrill of the first peacetime Christmas to enjoy in years? People were just so tickled to be putting lights on their trees again, and the song *I'll Be Home for Christmas* stopped being a sad dream.

But in those first few months after the war ended she was pregnant as well as on the verge of divorce. And even though she never owned up to any worries about living at home alone with her mother in such a sad state of affairs, she must have felt some unease about things because she took a stand with Bill on the divorce—she made up her mind that it wouldn't happen until after the baby was born. My mother always held to an unperturbed, almost blasé attitude when those times were brought up by anybody who ever wondered how it was for her. It must have been a tough spell—to be stuck at home, living in a little town of under a thousand people with a divorced mother when she was pregnant, poor, and almost divorced herself. But like so many other times in her life, she remained vague about how things were and never admitted that any of it bothered her. Maybe, as she always said, it was the times, and her peculiar optimism came from the excitement of the war ending—everybody was just so happy. And then there was always the chance that a knight in shining armor might come along to save the day for her.

Twelve

I don't want realism, I want magic!

—TENNESSEE WILLIAMS

When Daddy knocked on my grandmother's door in the spring of 1946 he was thirty-four years old. He'd been out of the army for only a few months, but it was long enough for him to know he wanted to get out of Mexico, Missouri, and away from his domineering older sisters and his grave and somber mother. He never failed to revere his mother, but any stories about Sophie Roth Clark always had the same thing in common—she was proper to the extreme. A favorite tale about her was that one time a friend was standing in front of their fireplace when the back of her dress caught on fire. Instead of letting the friend know right away that she was going up in flames, Sophie politely waited for her to be done talking before she told her about it.

"I didn't want to interrupt her," Sophie said later. Whether it was true or not, the story was typical of how she was described.

During his teenage years Daddy had picked up a bad reputation around their hometown, so after the war he decided to make a new start away from Mexico—he was ready to branch out because living in England had opened up the world to him. Serving in the Eighth Air Force in London was a big accomplishment, and he'd seen it through all on his own without any help from the family; his time in the service had given him a newfound self-confidence. The days of two older sisters controlling him needed to be over; they might be smarter and more sophisticated, but they'd never been to Europe and hadn't won a war.

Unlike so many others who went through the war, he was always happy to talk about the assignment he'd had in England with the landing crew of a ground force, and he loved the excitement of his job—rushing to bombers that had crash-landed after their raids on German forces. Bombers were often packed with two to three thousand gallons of high-octane gasoline plus bombloads that could explode at any minute. He and his team had to rescue any injured men and salvage the planes as best they could without any fatalities. The Eighth was equipped to send two thousand bombers on combat missions at a time, and they dropped on average a ton of bombs every minute from August 1942 to the end of the war.

Cyrus F. Clark Jr., circa 1942

Born by the River

Coming home, he felt like he had done something worthy of his family for the first time in his life, and that gave him the courage to move away from Mexico. The family farm in southern Missouri was tailor-made for a new life. The island was a four-hour drive south, so it was far enough away to get some independence but not too far for a quick trip home to check on his mother. Farming was something he knew about because he'd worked on some of the family farms around the county, plus the island had the added benefit of being perfect for a young man who liked to hunt whenever he had the chance. But as he made his plans and talked to people around town, it became clear to everybody that it was the legendary stories about hunting on the island that excited him more than the farming. Every year, for as long as any of them could remember, men from Mexico had gone down there to hunt, and they always came back with tales of ideal shooting grounds. On an average year, fifty ducks were bagged, and deer were plentiful. For Daddy, the island had everything.

His army buddy, Frank Armistead, was ready for a change too and was happy to go along for the ride, so together they made plans to move down to the island and start a new life. After transporting all their equipment overland from Mexico to the Mississippi River, the two of them set out on a barge loaded with gear from a little sandbar just south of Hannibal. They floated down the river for over two hundred miles on a spring runoff of high water and big dreams. During the next two weeks they reveled in the peacefulness of the Mississippi while they planned their new lives—then they came around a bend in the river and saw Grand Tower. Daddy knew it was the right spot when he looked over to the Missouri side of the river and saw the massive Tower Rock looming ahead. The two men had finally made it to the island.

At that time the three-thousand-acre farm was just about all that was left of the Clark family enterprises that in its heyday had included a bank, a thriving horse business, several rental houses, and hundreds of acres of farmland around Audrain County. In fact, the island that my grandfather, Cyrus F. Clark, had gotten in a trade for one of his famous Saddlebred Horses in 1914 was such a trifling part of the Clark holdings that he'd never even set foot on it. From the beginning C. F. Clark had leased it out instead of farming it himself, and for many years, my mother's grandfather, Frank Wilson, had worked it for him. Now Daddy was taking over, so it was only natural for him to check in with the Wilsons in Grand Tower since they knew a lot more about the island than he did. But the five Wilson boys were quick to cast a skeptical eye over him because he was, after all, the youngest son of the great Cyrus F. Clark—a man so revered by their own father, Grandpa Wilson, that one of them was even named after him. Although the Wilson brothers always said they loved the childhood years spent living on the island, you knew that Grandma and Grandpa Wilson had driven them really hard. The Wilson sons were skeptical that this young man, a Clark, thought he could manage the island where they had lived and worked for so many years—breaking their backs, clearing land, and farming under the domination of their poorly tempered parents. And his heavy drinking didn't impress them much either since for them life was about keeping your head down and your nose clean. Here was a man who'd had everything handed on a platter to him his whole life and came from a world that knew presidents and senators—where women rang a bell for servants, and the finest horses in the country were waiting in a world famous stable. It was all very suspicious to them and his flourishing manners with their older sister, Lola, and her deserted and pregnant daughter, Marion, were something they'd never seen up close before either. None of it made sense to their practical nature and being Missourians at heart, they would have to see his worth to believe it.

On the other hand, the people of Grand Tower, Illinois, weren't as wary of Cyrus Clark Jr. They had never heard much about the Clark family, so to them Cyrus Clark Sr. was just a rich man who used to own a big island two miles south of town that you had to take a boat to; it was even in another state. Mostly, they were just curious about the family, and their curiosity opened the door for my dad to become part of their tightly knit community. The war was over, and things were changing, so it made perfect sense that a wealthy young man from up north wanted to live in their ideal little town. Grand Tower had a proud history, and anything could happen now that there was peace and prosperity in the land.

Plus, he was friendly and seemed to shine with natural charisma. Cy appeared to have a generous nature and a deep respect for everybody no matter who they were or what they did for a living. And in spite of all the rumors about his rich family, he didn't seem to think he was better than the rest of the townspeople. Why, he even treated the town drunk fairly—he had given him a horse that was smart enough to find his way home when they picked the old man up off the tavern floor and put him in his wagon. And in no time at all he'd starting courting the Poe girl—a local WAC veteran who was pregnant and abandoned by her own husband after the war. He was young, handsome, and rich—and he was putting down roots faster than you could say "Jack Robinson."

After they met for the second time, their courtship moved along pretty fast even though Mother was six months pregnant with my sister. Around a small town like Grand Tower there isn't much that goes unnoticed. After a month, the news of their engagement was all over town and had found its way up to Mexico, where his widowed mother, Sophie Roth Clark, began to worry. She was seventy-seven in 1946, and by that time her husband, Cyrus Senior, had been dead for twelve years.

My grandmother had made it through the end of the Depression and the war years without her husband, but she wasn't ready for her only son to leave home and then become engaged to a pregnant woman who was still married. He was the only man in her family, and she clung to the idea that someday he would amount to something—Sophie was holding out hope that her son would rebuild the family business interests. The memory of her own father, Adam Roth, reigning over his grocery supply company in Saint Louis, even into old age, was her idea of how things should work. For Sophie, it seemed long past time to lean on her three children for help with the more troublesome parts of life, but each one of them was busy developing their own ideas—ideas that didn't include Mexico, Missouri.

Clark house in Mexico, Missouri

Sophie's oldest daughter and my father's sister, Margaretha, was easygoing. But Mother always said she liked being with her friends more than she ever thought about the family. After Margaretha graduated from Lindenwood College in 1929, she moved to Saint Louis where she worked at the Stix, Baer and Fuller department store. She was having a good time going out with her Roth cousins and boys from Washington University, but there was pressure from home over money because she wasn't making enough to support herself. When their bank failed and the Depression hit hard, the Clark family was in dire straits. She reluctantly gave up her life in Saint Louis after a year and a half of living in the city and moved back home to Mexico to take a job, teaching in a school. Then, in 1932 she did something that changed her life forever—she went to visit her mother's younger sister, Beulah Roth Barker, in Banning, California, for the summer.

Margaretha Clark was twenty-four years old and ready for adventure when she caught the train in Missouri bound for California. Although her parents sent her off with good wishes, the excitement of her letters from the Golden State took them by surprise. When she wrote home that there were three boys for every girl in California, her father, C. F. Clark, wrote back with some advice in case she fell in love: "Now, my daughter, if you should get California-struck, use the same wisdom your aunt used and have him come to your home and have your mother and best friends look him over, and it may be safe. I cannot say." He was referring to her aunt Beulah, who'd met her future husband, Charles Omar Barker, in California when the Roths had gone there on vacation in 1904.

But it wasn't just the California boys that swept her away. After another enthusiastic letter home about the wonders of the state, her dad was bewildered. He wrote back to her: "I was really surprised that you had to use so many superlatives to describe everything that came under your view. Nothing could be described in the nominative or comparative degree. But is nothing short of the superlative degree [sic] would suit you in your description of California and its products. I really don't see how that can be. I have been in California two or three times, but truly I have never seen anything there to go wild over." But he hadn't been to California in over fifty years, and at eighty-four, it was hard to imagine he understood much about what his twenty-four-year-old daughter was feeling.

Her adventurous time in California was a life-altering trip, but it quickly came to an end. The summer was over, and it was time for her to come home to Mexico and go back to her teaching job. A year later, she wrote a letter to her aunt Beulah, "This time last year, I was in California. Every day I have thought this time last year I was doing this or that thing and how much pleasure I derived from each minute of my visit."

Because the two sisters' families, the Barkers and the Clarks, had so much in common, Margaretha felt at home with her California kin from the start. The fortunes of both families had started out with farming and then moved on to state politics and banking. In 1893, Beulah Roth Barker's future husband, Representative Charles O. Barker, introduced the bill to create Riverside County in the California State Assembly, and a few years later in 1899, Sophie's future husband, Representative Cyrus F. Clark, proposed the bill to create the Missouri State Fair in the Missouri State Legislature. Like most politicians, both men stood to benefit from their work in government. Charles Barker managed to take control of the water rights in the area—something he held on to until 1934—while back in Missouri, C. F. Clark used the state fair to showcase his championship thoroughbred horses.

The Clark and Barker families had a lot in common before the Depression, but the 1930s had different effects on the two families. The Barkers weathered the Depression a lot better than the Clarks—with their ranches, canneries, and a bank still intact. Back in Missouri, the prosperity of the Clark family was vanishing. For Margaretha, the Barkers laid bare what life should have been like in her own family. Instead of her contentious and bossy sister and her ne'er-do-well brother, the Barkers were achievers who knew how to relax and have good time. Money remained easy for them, and her aunt Beulah wasn't as formal and religious as her own mother, Sophie. The whole family was more lighthearted. As the years passed, Margaretha sorely missed the lively Barkers with their carefree attitudes—plus she was more social than the rest of her family back home in Mexico, so the California cousins made an everlasting impression on her. But if Margaretha was making any plans to move to California, the failing health and death of her father in 1934 put a temporary end to her dreams. A year later in 1935 she managed to go back for graduate school at the University of Southern California, but after that and through the war years, she lived in Mexico and taught at the local school. As she reconnected with childhood friends around town everyone expected her to find a husband, but that was easier said than done during the Depression and the war. Then Lakenan Barnes came home to Mexico for the summer, and California lost some of its luster.

Anybody would have said that Lakenan Barnes and Margaretha Clark were tailor-made for each other. Cyrus F. Clark's first wife was descended from the Barnes clan, so the families were old friends if not kin. Lakenan had grown up in one of the oldest families in town and was educated at Amherst College, the University of Missouri, the University of Virginia, and Harvard. When he returned home during school breaks and over the summers, the two of them cultivated a detached, uncommitted style of romance that suited both their independent personalities. The war years passed easily enough with her teaching in Mexico and him serving, but after it was over he stayed on in Tokyo with the occupation forces and was in no hurry to come home to get married. But even through those times they kept up their courtship—he wrote often and regularly sent her valuable Japanese treasures that were more like the spoils of war than gifts from a beau. For a few years he lived with two other army officers in a small period house just outside the gates of the beautiful Fujiya Hotel in Hakone while he served and collected antiques for himself and his friends and family back home. Oftentimes he and the other officers had their meals in the hotel dining room—you can hear the longing for those days in his words as he recalled the elegant room in a letter he wrote years later, "The high crisscrossed ceiling beams had small lights at each of the many intersections so that the table glassware, reflecting and refracting so many light sources, contributed to a note of glittering elegance." It seems like he went through life pining more for his bygone days in Japan than any lost opportunities to get married, but eventually he did come back to Mexico and took up with the family law practice. By the time he died, he'd published poetry and quips in the *Wall Street Journal, Reader's Digest,* and the *Saturday Evening Post.* In the end, neither he nor Margaretha ever married, and Lakenan died in the house where he was born at 724 South Jefferson in Mexico, Missouri. It was the only legal address he ever had.

Thirteen

*Everyone is a moon, and has a dark side
which he never shows to anybody.*

—MARK TWAIN

It seemed like the family was right when they said
Margaretha cared more about her friends than anyone
else, but that was a blessing compared to her sister's smothering ways. Elizabeth Jenness Clark, the middle child in the
family, always had to have her finger in everybody's pie and
never thought for a minute about sitting back to enjoy a
peaceful time that wasn't about either learning or suffering.
She found it hard to consider another person's opinion or
to think they might have their own way of doing something,
and it always felt like she thought any idea not set by her was
foolish. All her life she seemed driven and focused.

Margaretha and Cy used to reminisce about the good
times they had when the Clark children spent their summers

at the Roth house in Bay View, Michigan, but Liz was never content there. She quickly found a vigorous camp nearby and returned to it every summer until she was in her midtwenties. Even into the family's lean years during the Depression, Liz moved heaven and earth to make sure she went back there every summer. She loved doing all the camping activities like hacking through the forest, sleeping out among the mosquitos on the hard ground, and fording rivers.

By the time World War II ended, both Liz and Margaretha were in their late thirties and had good jobs. Like their mother, Sophie, they'd graduated from Lindenwood College, and later on in life they both earned graduate degrees—Liz in social work from Washington University in Saint Louis and Margaretha in education from the University of Missouri. But like so many of their Roth aunts, neither one of them was showing any signs of getting married, and time was slipping by—it was becoming more and more clear that the family legacy was all on their brother's shoulders. He would have to get married and have children.

But Cy had always been trouble, and he was never on track for settling down. His father was sixty-three when he was born, and even though Cyrus Sr. lived another twenty-three years to raise him into manhood, the age difference was a big drawback to how they got along. The old New England Puritan had a warm and loving side, and he never stopped believing his youngest son would turn his life around, but his letters from those times reveal that his hope was fading. In January of 1929 when Cy was struggling through his sophomore year of high school Cyrus Sr. wrote to his daughter, Margaretha, while she was away at college: "He does not seem to know how to study and I do not think he tries much. I guess you know what that means."

Letters during the school year were always full of worry, but in the summer, Cy got glowing reports from his father about the odd jobs he held around town—especially his work on the farms.

A year later, in another letter to Margaretha, Cyrus wrote about a conviction he held fast to—the belief that your legacy and reputation meant something. He wrote, "The tombstones out in the graveyard show where many of my loved ones lie; but thank God they all left honorable histories behind. I am not ashamed of the history of a single one of them. This is a heritage to be proud of. I hope the same can be said of each one of my children and that they have been a blessing to mankind and that the world was made better on their account."

Since his two daughters were doing pretty well in life at the time he wrote those words, it's not hard to imagine he was thinking about Cy's future, but none of these worries were made any easier by his youngest son's drinking. Cy was fourteen when he had his first drink, and I heard him say once that he knew right away it was just what he needed to feel normal. So that meant his father endured eight long years between Cy's first drink and his own death in 1934 at the age of eighty-seven. Before Cy's junior year in high school, they managed to move him into the Catholic school in town, and everyone was thrilled when he finally graduated in 1931, but it was a year later than most of his friends. Cy was well liked around town, though—he always got along with people and was able to find jobs, but he showed no signs of ambition or interest in getting an education like his sisters. He drank too much and had a bad habit of going too far—especially on the night when he got married while he was on a binge. Luckily the girl cooperated with the family, and the Clarks were able to get their marriage annulled.

In the summer of 1946, when the troubling news hit Mexico that Cy was engaged to a married, pregnant woman, the whole family went into an uproar; the story was especially troubling when they recalled his marriage history. Sophie's doctor was worried about her heart, since she was suffering from high blood pressure, so he advised her to stay calm and get extra rest. At the time Liz was working in Booneville, Missouri, as a social worker, and Margaretha was teaching in Mexico. Since Margaretha had the summer off, Sophie quickly decided that she should go down to Grand Tower to look into the situation. Of her two daughters, Margaretha was the friendliest and the most agreeable, so Sophie hoped she would find something positive in all this business.

Both Margaretha and her mother thought that Liz should be kept as far away from Cy as possible. The family had been dealing with Liz and Cy's dislike for each other since they were young, so when he went off track it always fell to Margaretha to step in and put things right—she always ran interference over her little brother. Cyrus Clark Sr. had written to her fifteen years earlier, "Your letters to Cy do him a lot of good. I really think that every letter he gets from you helps him. I think Cy really loves you more than he does Elizabeth, and I think that is one of the reasons why your letters help him so much."

Margaretha Arnold Clark and her mother,
Sophia Margaretha Roth Clark, circa 1945

Sophie knew Liz would only start trouble with her controlling and confrontational ways, and she felt that if Cy knew what Liz was saying about him, he might end up marrying this woman just to spite her; it wouldn't have been the first time Cy did something stupid because Liz told him not to. Nobody was surprised when Liz raised the roof after she heard the news; she quickly pointed out that her little brother always had to play the part of a knight in shining armor.

"He can never resist helping an underdog; it's a pattern of behavior in him," she announced when she heard about the engagement. "And he drinks too much. He needs to be in an alcoholic treatment program."

Sophie cringed at the newfangled notions about psychology that Liz had picked up in graduate school; in her opinion those kinds of ideas only made everything worse. She didn't understand the new theories about people's behavior, and she certainly didn't like the thought of somebody in her family discussing their personal problems with a stranger. Sophie was a Roth, and the only way you were supposed to deal with your difficulties was to pretend they didn't exist and then live your life the way you would have done anyway.

Plus, she didn't have time to study the situation—she had to try to put an end to it. So notes were quickly written about the visit on engraved stationery from Mexico and answered back with notebook paper from Grand Tower. When

Liz read Marion's letter she threw it down onto her mother's desk with a smirk—there was nothing more to be said about the whole mess; this horribly written letter on such crude stationary said it all.

But things went forward—a day was picked, and the details were arranged so that by the time of the visit everybody in both towns knew about it. Margaretha's plan was to drive straight down to Grand Tower so she would be there by twelve or one o'clock and then head back up to Saint Louis to spend the night. It would be a little over six hours driving by the time she was done, which was a lot of time in the car, but now that school was out it was a good excuse to do some shopping and spend some time with her cousin Eleanor Price.

Although she was willing to make the trip, Margaretha wasn't as concerned about Cy as her mother and sister because like most people after the war, she was busy making big plans of her own. Once again her mind was full of California, and she was planning on moving there as soon as possible. By then she was thirty-seven years old and done waiting for a proposal from Lakenan or anyone else. "I like men all right," she would say, "but I wouldn't want one around the house all the time."

For her, the burning desire to go to California was more important than getting married, and it could not wait another year even though she would be leaving her mother alone in Mexico at the age of seventy-seven. Margaretha had spent the war years taking care of Sophie while her brother was in England and her sister, Liz, was working on her career, so she felt like it was her turn to get out of Mexico. One quick visit down to see the island at Grand Tower was no big deal, and since one third of it would be hers after her mother died, she needed to take an interest. She would do this for her mother and then break the news to her about California.

Unlike Margaretha, Marion was excited about the meeting, especially since it was an official visit from one of Cy's sisters. For her, the upcoming social call was meaningful because it promised to be a glimpse into the new life she would be leading as his wife. In her mind, she saw things for herself changing into the more glamorous and refined lifestyle that she'd seen at relatives' homes in Saint Louis and Dallas during the war. As she hurried around her mother's house trying to figure out how to manage things, she felt a little put out by Cy's casual take on everything. He wasn't offering any advice, and all he could say was to thank God that it was Margaretha coming down instead of Liz and that Margaretha was the best one in the whole family.

Marion had no idea that the Clarks were uneasy about their wedding plans, and if Cy knew, he didn't let on. After all, at thirty-four, he probably felt like it was none of their business—especially Liz's. He wasn't worried about their approval, and that made Marion all the more confident of his loyalty to her. She never knew they were looking her over, and it's easy to understand why she was in the dark. Even though her mother was embarrassed by her own divorce and she herself would be divorced in a few months, Marion had every reason to be proud of her roots. Her relatives were part of two large and well-respected families in Grand Tower and Cape Girardeau. Both the Poes and the Wilsons were good people—even the best in the area. Her uncle was a doctor in Dallas, her grandfather owned his own farm, and another uncle and her father were both riverboat pilots. There was nothing more impressive than those professions along the Mississippi.

But Cy's family was not from those parts. He was a descendent of New England Puritans and German immigrants who had built-up small business empires, not Southerners who'd migrated from Virginia or rivermen. The education and cultural differences of their two families were as different as the financial ones. But Marion wasn't aware of any of this. She knew Cy's family came from more money than hers, and from going to the movies she understood they probably lived differently, but she had no reason to think that his family might consider her beneath them. She was from a good family, and he was from a very good family—under the rigid social rules in her part of the country the two could marry. Her extended family and tightly knit community gave her the confidence to be excited and positive about her upcoming marriage. And since her grandfather had worked for Cyrus F. Clark Sr., she already felt connected to them.

Marion's main concern was how to show her future sister-in-law, Margaretha, that she could manage the role of Cy's wife. Her confidence made her want to prove that she would seamlessly fit in with the Clarks at a time when it might have been better for her to think twice about what was about to happen. Instead, her usual blasé, devil-may-care attitude was getting caught up with the vague dreams she had about her new life. Her future sister-in-law, Margaretha, was coming for "lunch"—it sounded so grand and official. Even the word itself seemed unusual since people in Grand Tower didn't even eat lunch and then dinner—for them it was dinner and supper. Dinner was the midday meal, not lunch. There were a lot of plans for her to mull over, but unfortunately she was thinking about all the wrong things.

Marion started to consider the rumors she had heard about the Clarks as she set about planning the event. Thinking back to the talk that had circled around the Wilson family over the past twenty years, she remembered they had a cook and a housekeeper, so she made up her mind that she needed to have servants as well. In the end, she formed a plan that her mother would stay in the kitchen and act as the cook filling that role and a local girl who was about twelve could be hired as a maid. Her mother would make chicken and dumplings—a meal that was everyone's favorite.

Born by the River

On the day of the meeting, Margaretha headed south from Mexico right after breakfast. The morning was already hot and humid, but she was dressed for it and with all the windows down, there was a little relief from the heat. She thought about her timing again—the most important thing about the whole day was to make it back to Saint Louis in time to go out to dinner with Eleanor. She had to be careful not to get lost, but with two state maps on the seat next to her and her notes from Cy's directions, she felt like the situation was in hand. He said to cross the bridge at Chester and then head south on Highway 3, turn right at the turnoff to Grand Tower, and follow the road straight over to the river. The town was at the end of the line. Then he said to turn right on Main Street and look for the white shotgun house about two blocks up on the right.

After crossing the river at Chester, she followed the Trail of Tears Highway until she saw a run-down sign pointing to Grand Tower—she almost missed it. By the time she made the turn, it was already one o'clock and hotter than hell.

As soon as she drove into Grand Tower, Margaretha was taken aback by how run-down everything looked, and before too long she was lost because there weren't many street signs. Getting lost didn't matter too much, though, since the town was so tiny—it only took her about ten minutes to drive up and down all the roads. Then she got distracted by thinking about how she'd only seen one decent house in the whole place—it was nice, but it looked more like a big, white riverboat than a regular home. She couldn't imagine where all the good people lived, and the entire town felt like the wrong side of the tracks back in Mexico. Front Street had some restaurants, a drugstore, and a bank. But it was shocking to see how close the Mississippi was—a large boat was going pretty fast downriver, and it looked bigger than the whole town. She'd never seen a place where people lived so near the Mississippi before; it seemed like nothing was keeping the river out of the town.

After driving around for a while, she realized that all Cy had said was a street name—he'd never mentioned a house number or told her what a shotgun house was. She dreaded the idea of asking someone for directions but couldn't think of what else to do. She slowed the car down when a man in dirty overalls stopped in the middle of the road and gawked at her with a bewildered look on his face. Before there was a chance to speak, though, he yelled out in a grumpy voice, "Who ya lookin' out fer?" She thought about locking the door but decided not to when she remembered that all the windows were down and, anyway, it might make him mad.

"The Wilsons," she said, not 100 percent sure. Wasn't that the name of the man who used to farm the island?

"Well, dar's only 'bout five different bunches of them." He started laughing like he'd told a joke.

"It's a shotgun house," she finally thought to say. Without a word, he pointed to a skinny little white house down the block.

The house he pointed out didn't seem right—it had to be the smallest one in the town, but she parked the car in front and walked up to the porch anyway. By the time she made it to the stairs, she realized that it was the right house—people suddenly seemed to come out of nowhere, and there was Cy grinning from ear to ear while he introduced her to everybody. Pretty soon there were at least seven of them standing on the little porch. She was hot and felt closed in, but nobody moved—they seemed content to stand there with their happy-go-lucky manner like they had all the time in the world. The heat and the shock of the place had given her a little jolt, but their easy ways didn't make things any better—it was as if she had been transported to a different world, and she felt like a fish out of water. All this friendliness was giving her an uneasy, claustrophobic feeling like they were smothering her in a blanket on a hot day.

Pretty soon, they were even teasing her. "You're late," someone said. "What happened—did you fall in the river?" They all chuckled. The Mississippi was close, so she could imagine that people did fall in, but they were all laughing like it was a big joke. She tried to explain how she couldn't find the house and about the man in the street, but then it came out that she didn't know what a shotgun house was.

They howled. Somebody tried to explain, but it didn't make any sense to her. Why would a house be designed so you could shoot a gun through the front door?

The answer, "So the bullet could go straight through and out the back without hitting anything," seemed just as confusing. But she didn't really care, so she nodded her head and wondered if anybody would ever offer her a place to sit.

Margaretha had never liked chicken and dumplings and didn't understand why Marion's mother, Mrs. Poe, stayed in the kitchen all through the luncheon. And it seemed odd to have a young girl, who was more like a child, standing off to the side of the porch with a broom. Every now and then the girl smiled foolishly and swept up the ashes that Marion casually flicked onto the floor; Margaretha looked around for an ashtray and wondered why they didn't have one.

By the time lunch was over, she felt like she couldn't wait to get out of there. As if things weren't bad enough, when she asked to use the bathroom before leaving they took her to a privy behind the house. Then something brown and furry ran out from underneath it when she opened the door. Once in the car, she drove out of town as fast as she could. But before the highway, she had to pull over and collect herself. Looking over at the map, her eyes started to follow the roads that led out west and straight through to California. She was amazed at how different California was from this place. *How could Cy think it was all right to live here?* It was so far from anything she could ever imagine herself doing that the idea of changing his mind about the marriage seemed more impossible than ever. She decided that if marrying this woman made her brother happy then so be it. Pulling back onto the highway, she reminded herself that all the people she'd just met were really very nice. "The salt of the earth," she said out loud. And having an instant family might even settle him down a little; after all, he couldn't have seemed happier or more content. She decided that the best thing to do was to keep the peace in the family and tell her mother that everything was fine. Liz would just have to lump it.

Fourteen

What, I ask you, is harmless about a dreamer...

—T<small>ENNESSEE</small> W<small>ILLIAMS</small>

*D*addy's truck finally came to stop in our front drive, and we slowly made our way into the house. Of course, we went to our beds right away, but I had trouble getting to sleep that night—the distant sound of our hound dogs baying was echoing across the island, and it was good to hear. I was home again after being gone for so many months, and sleep seemed like a waste of time—it was more fun to imagine what I would do in the morning—being back home was the best thing in the world. To be in my own bed and see my toys and books again was like eating hushpuppies, fudge, and hand-churned ice cream all at the same time. Tomorrow there might be pink, fluffy clouds hanging over the horse pasture, and at night I could go outside and look at the stars if I wanted to.

Just walking into my bedroom and closing the door was a treat for me because I'd passed so many long weeks in places where it was hard to find a spot to have my own thoughts or to play in peace. During all those nights at different relatives' houses in town, at Aunt Liz's house, or even at Grandpa Wilson's farm, I always had the same sorrowful longing— *please just let me go home.* And it was around this time that another level of feeling about the island was starting to add to my love of home—I was just beginning to understand the remarkable place where we lived. Now that I was old enough, I could venture out and ride my bike down the dirt roads of the island; I could follow tractor paths back into the woods and look around to see all the wonderful hidden places that were there. Sometimes, I rode down to the sandbar along the chute and found patches of grass where deer slept or climbed to the other side of the levee and walked down the dirt road to the river. My surroundings were starting to take a strong hold on me with a power that has never really let up in all the years since.

As I lay awake, I thought about asking Daddy to tell me a ghost story like he did so often, but it didn't seem like he'd want to since it was so late. Now that I was thinking about a story, though, some of them were stuck in my mind, and it was hard to get them out.

I don't know why I loved them so much since they never failed to scare the living daylights out of me. He never told a story the way most people did—by having it be about something that happened to somebody else or like a tale from a book. He always told a story like it was a real event from his own life with people and places that I already knew about. By then I was old enough to know they weren't really things that had happened to him—he hadn't ever been trapped in an underground cavern by a man who slowly walled him in by laying bricks over the door, and I knew that he'd never ridden through a cemetery and seen a headless horseman. But for years I believed those things really happened to him. He would start out the story with something like, "One cold winter night, when I was riding through the cemetery in Mexico on our old burrow, Pete, all of a sudden the moon came out from behind the clouds."

My favorite one was about the time he'd gone to see an old friend whose sister was sick. They thought she died and then accidently buried her alive. But she escaped from her tomb and came back to walk around and scare them. Then the house fell in as Daddy was riding off on his horse. Daddy turned around to see the creepy old building crumble and knew that everybody inside was dead. It was the end of his friend, Robert Usher's whole family—all the people and their home were gone forever. It was awful to think about—a whole family perished.

Pretty soon, I started doing what I always did after Daddy told me a story—I started thinking about the scary faces on the knobs of my dresser. I squinted my eyes to see if I could make them out, but it was too dark. Maybe tomorrow I'd look in the back of the drawers again to see if there was any more jewelry stuffed back in there. I'd found a lot of things in it over the years, but I never thought to ask who used to own them—probably somebody on the Roth side. I hoped they wouldn't come back from the dead to look for their treasures—I'd never thought to worry about the possibility of that happening before.

Fifteen

*There is a time for departure even when
there's no certain place to go.*

—Tennessee Williams

It's common practice for people to make up a story about someone and then fall in love with that fantasy instead of seeing the real person. I think that's what both my parents did from the beginning. When Cy first met Marion she was in the middle of her pregnancy surrounded by a big extended family in a place where a lot of people were ready to look up to him—probably for the first time in his life. She was pretty and vivacious, and he felt an immediate connection to her because of her people's strong history on the island. Marion was from a family that had been farming for as far back as anybody could remember, and so it was easy for him to think she'd know how to be a farmer's wife. What he didn't see, though, was that while her grandfather was a farmer, her own father was a riverboat captain—that was the world she'd grown up in, not on a farm. Marion, on the other hand, saw him as a handsome, almost courtly gentleman who came from another world and was like no one she'd ever met. His family was idolized by her grandfather, and although she didn't remember meeting him before, her mother did, so they quickly saw each other as old acquaintances. They were ready to feel like things were meant to be, and in 1946, it was easy to fall in love. The two images they had of each other would have fit together perfectly if they'd both accepted their own true natures—he was a gentleman farmer, not a dirt farmer. And in the end she may not have been a very good cook or known how to keep chickens, but she was always content to stay at home and lose herself in the fantasy world of a book; living out in the middle of nowhere wouldn't have bothered her too much. But their main differences, in the end, came from their family backgrounds that were poles apart—his family was from New England and Germany, and hers hailed from Virginia, Tennessee, and North Carolina. When things started to go south in their marriage, it always felt like they didn't speak the same language. They were two people whose ways didn't match.

After my sister was born in June, Marion got her divorce from Bill Paul. On October 26, 1946, my mother and father were married at the Jackson County Courthouse. The first few years of their life together, when they were living across the street from Grandma in town, were happy enough. During the day, Daddy would go down to the island to work the logging business he'd started with his old army buddy, Frank, and Uncle Shorty, one of the Wilson brothers. At first, they floated the logs downriver to a sawmill in Cape Girardeau, and then later he built his own mill on the island and started cutting lumber that was hauled off on a barge. At night, he would go to the taverns around Grand Tower, but he always came home. Mother was content to be surrounded by her friends and family.

But things were about to change. In 1949 the US Army Corps of Engineers was building a levee in front of Grand Tower and decided it would be easier to build it across the island rather than around it. Under the plan, two thousand acres of the island would be protected from flooding, and one thousand acres would serve as a buffer for the levee on the riverside. The value of some of the most fertile river-bottom land in the country would skyrocket once it was safe from flooding. The offer wasn't something the family could ignore. But there was a big catch to the plan—the army engineers wouldn't build the levee over the island unless somebody lived on it—and at that time it was uninhabited. So Marion and Cy, along with my three-year-old sister, left their house in town and moved into the leaky old building Frank Wilson had built on the island in the 1920s. It was originally made to be a schoolhouse for the Wilson sons who were taught by their older sister, my grandma, before she married Wamp Poe—it was never supposed to be a place to live. There was no electricity, generator, telephone, or indoor toilet, so it was cold, wet, and drafty. It had all those inconveniences, plus you were living on an island in the Mississippi River. But Cy and Marion were ready for the challenge and went into it with an open heart. Both sets of Marion's parents had lived on the island when they worked for the Clarks—her parents had even fallen in love and started their family on the island, and her sister Nettie was born there. It was just as much a part of her family history as it was Cy's—she was following her roots, and he was following his dreams.

Cyrus F. Clark Jr. on the island, circa 1947

Yet it seemed like they would never get the life she craved because after they moved, Cy wasn't ready to give up his friends in town. He would go into Grand Tower for business or supplies and then go for a drink. Often he stayed the night, and sometimes he would leave on Friday night and not come back until Monday morning. A farmhand and his wife were living off and on in another house that was about half a mile away, but most of the time my mother and sister were left alone on the island.

When I asked her what it must have been like, she would keep to her usual blasé attitude and talk about going into town and bringing back loads of books from the Grand Tower bookmobile. She also liked to think back to the funny things that happened on the island like one time when the wagon got stuck, and they fell into the mud. When I pressed her about his drinking, she would offer up the resigned attitude a wife needed during those times—women didn't have many options back then, she would say, and she still loved him and always thought he loved her, too. Besides, once the levee was built they would have a road into Grand Tower, and then she wouldn't be so stuck. All this was tolerable enough until rumors started to fly around town that Cy had a girlfriend.

The story was that the other woman was from the wrong side of the tracks and married to a man who didn't care if she went out on him—Marion knew her from high school. Pretty soon talk about them was common around town, and it was awful for her. The worst thing about it, she said, was that people started to "make cracks" to her when she went into Grand Tower. It was a small town of under a thousand people, so nothing was private. The situation was embarrassing, but she held on to the idea that if they had a child he would settle down. Those hopes started to fade after a couple of miscarriages, but things got better when she finally carried a child to term and they moved into town to give birth. But I was a girl, so now there was another reason to have a drink. Pretty soon, she was back on the island in the old routine of him being gone and hearing the rumors again. Now, though, her life was a lot harder because she had a five-year-old and a newborn, and it would be some time before the levee was finished. Around this time, Cy adopted my sister, so that boosted her spirits enough to keep her holding on.

When I was about two, the road on top of the levee was finally done, and we could drive off and on the island. Using lumber from the sawmill, Cy and Frank Armistead built a bigger house with indoor plumbing, so we were able to have a regular home. Things really looked up when they bought a generator from an army surplus store—now we were finally done with kerosene lamps. Several farmhands were hired, so more people were around, and it wasn't as lonely. With the levee, the farm started taking off, and Cy was busy farming a few hundred of the thousand acres that were cleared—the rest of it was leased out to a tenant farmer. Then they hired Myrtle Black to be a housekeeper, and most of the time Mom, as we always called her, lived on the island with us. Marion's life improved, but nothing changed with the thorn that was hurting her the most—the girlfriend in town. She tried to turn to his sisters for help, but it seemed like they wouldn't believe their brother was capable of having a girlfriend. They knew about the drinking—he had done that in Mexico since he was a teenager—but going out with another woman was not something they would accept. It didn't help that Liz was always ready to find fault with the sister-in-law she'd disliked from the beginning—blaming Marion was a lot easier than her brother even though he drank too much and behaved foolishly. The problem, according to Liz, was Marion.

Things didn't improve with the levee because Cy was gone more than ever, and most nights she was still alone. Then she lost the support of her mother when she moved across the river to take care of Grandpa and Grandma Wilson. Others in the family saw the writing on the wall and started encouraging her to leave him, but she stayed. She was treading water and barely staying afloat. I was about four when she heard about the GI Bill and how it would pay for her to go to college—with that in mind, she could finally see a way out. When I started grade school, she enrolled at Southern Illinois University in Carbondale, which was about twenty-five miles from our house. Once there, her world opened up, and she was able to meet other people her own age who had been through the war and were on the same track. And since she loved reading and learning about new things, she enjoyed the academics of her major in education. For more than one reason, the campus became a refuge for her.

Life continued on in the same way while she drove back and forth for four years to go to college. We spent every Christmas with Aunt Liz in Topeka, Kansas, and when I was old enough, I passed most of my summers on Grandpa Wilson's farm across the river in Missouri. Daddy kept seeing his girlfriend in town, but with Mother's eyes on a way out of the marriage, she became less tolerant and started to confront him about other things. Her college friends and the new world in Carbondale were quickly opening up her eyes. The comments by the townspeople only got worse when she started school, though, because a woman going to college wasn't a common thing, but by this time she'd moved on from small-town gossip. If she could just hold on long enough, things would work out for her.

Sixteen

Where does one go from a world of insanity?
Somewhere on the other side of despair.

—T. S. ELIOT

That September marked the last time I would start school from the island. I would never again walk over to the barn at the other end of the horse pasture, ride my bike down to the chute, or walk into my bedroom and close the door. And it would also be the last time we would live together as a family.

By then, I'd already stopped being able to ignore what was going on—you couldn't get away from all the bad. Arguments started to become a regular part of our lives, and I remember thinking, *Could you please just stop?*

One day, all of a sudden, it did stop. Mother came into my room and said, "You always wanted to move to town, so we're moving to town. Start packing." I tried to tell her that I never really wanted to move, but it didn't seem to matter.

When we moved, that was the day I slipped overboard—I didn't know it then, but Daddy had already fallen in.

Aunt Liz had managed to have him declared incompetent because of his drinking, and Aunt Margaretha had gone along with it—then they sold the island. Aunt Liz's years of working in mental health in Missouri had paid off for her—she knew the right people and was able to fix things the way she wanted. But now I know, as I look back, that all four of them were to blame for what happened—Aunt Liz for her need to control everything, Aunt Margaretha because of her indifference, Mother with her blasé, devil-may-care attitude that she always threw in their faces, and of course Daddy for his never-ending ability to make the wrong decisions, his drinking, and his idealistic ways. None of their dreams ever came true, and it was their own fault.

My mother, my sister, and I moved up north to a town in the middle of a flat cornfield; it had ten thousand people, and I felt overwhelmed living so close to all of them. There were no hills, no bluffs, and no rivers there. None of the women carried baskets of work around with them, sat in rocking chairs, or cooked chicken and dumplings; none of the men had soft cackling laughs, wore overalls, or set catfish nets. Overnight all the people who had filled my life slipped away from me—all the aunts, uncles, and cousins were gone. Grandpa Wilson died five years later, but we didn't even go to his funeral. After his death, my grandma moved back into her old house in Grand Tower, but then she died a year later. I don't ever remember visiting her even once after the island was sold. Mother retreated into her books, and Daddy moved away to find work. We saw him once or twice a year for a few days around the holidays, but he had the same faraway look in his eyes he'd had when he came to pick me up at Grandma's on that last day of summer. Only this time it never went away, and he was thereafter a broken man.

I spent the next fifteen years fighting as hard as I could against the currents and the whirlpools that were trying pull me under. Mostly I floated facedown with my hair drifting around my body in the way that Uncle Price had foretold. Finally, after a long time of struggling, I was able to crawl up onto dry land and put my life back together. I guess there was something left in me from that place and those people who lived along the river. It gave me enough strength and good sense to know I had to keep swimming.

The End

About the Author

Jenness Clark grew up on an island in the Mississippi River that was owned and farmed by her family.

She graduated from the University of Washington and currently lives in Seattle with her husband. They have two children.